TASTEFULLY
Yours

BETTY THIESSEN

TASTEFULLY YOURS
A Collection of My Finest Recipes

Published by:

WORD ALIVE PRESS

131 Cordite Road
Winnipeg, Manitoba, Canada R3W 1S1
Phone: (866) 967-3782 (Toll-free in North America)
Phone: (204) 777-7100 (International)

ISBN 1-894928-68-7

Cover Photo by Jon Schroeder

Cover and Interior Design by Nikki Braun

Printed in Canada

Distributed by Word Alive Press

Introduction

This is updated new edition of my favourite recipes. No cookbook fills all our needs. If there were such a book, I would have it, rather than the stacks in my cupboards. This is not meant to be a basic all-purpose meal planner, but is a collection of recipes that supplement our basic "meat and potatoes" recipes.

In the first book I published, I concentrated on gourmet recipes that I like. Since then, I discovered my Mom's old recipe file and found some good old stand-bys like Tapioca Pudding, Macaroon Cake, and Basic Sponge Cake, etc. We always thought that the last generation ate a lot of fatty food, which was true in part, but the desserts are simple and many are low-fat.

Some of the recipes I've included use wine in the cooking. If you prefer, you can use non-alcoholic wine, available in the grocery store, (although, you can rest assured that the alcohol content of the wine is cooked out of the food). I often use cooking wine, also available in the grocery store, mostly because it's easy access. Cooking with wine brings a rich flavour to many dishes and adds that special touch when company is expected.

Why develop the art of cooking? The best time to begin cooking is as a child. My mom was often sick, so I got to experiment and cook when I was quite young. I thank my Junior High Home Economics teacher, Miss Helen Janzen, for teaching me the basics of cooking, and for being a great inspiration.

The kitchen is a place where the family can have fun working together with a cheerful attitude. I believe that a mom with a positive attitude in serving her family good wholesome meals will aid in the growth of her children, and will even bring added security to the family.

The running of a home and the preparation of food is creative. This is something that too often is missed entirely in the education of our children. Our increasing intellectualized society places little value on the satisfaction and fulfillment received from placing a nutritious and attractive meal on the table, without strain.

I believe it is important to economize and have a food budget. Use fruits and vegetables in season when planning your menus. I try to be careful to see that leftovers are used in the most creative way possible.

BE HOSPITABLE

Many people are afraid of extending hospitality. They have only one or two standard recipes for company. Try a new dish and enjoy the adventure of new taste sensations.

Quin Sherrer and Laura Watson, in their book: "A House of Many Blessings," define hospitality as "reaching out to those God puts in your path." I believe that it is a must for all Christians. When we show love to one another in this way, we are showing our love for God.

"Cheerfully share your home with those who need a meal or a place to stay." I Peter 4:9

The Bible speaks a lot about hospitality and even lists it as a requirement for qualifying to be an elder! Don't wait until you have a perfect home or lots of time to practice hospitality. God wants us to "live to give" as Wayne Meyers puts it. Whatever God has given you, keep your heart and hands open to extend those blessings to others so they will be blessed.

I hope you enjoy these recipes and share them with friends. They are gleaned from magazines, cookbooks, and friends, but with my own original variations and changes.

Thanks to family and friends that have shared their recipes with me.

Bon Appetit! Enjoy,

Betty Thiessen

Setting the Table

Whether you are setting a table for the family or for company, it is good to set it properly.

Plates and cutlery are set about one inch from the edge of the table. The cutlery is set according to the order it is used from the outside in.

The knife should have the sharp edge turned in toward the plate.

The salad and/or bread and butter plate is placed above the fork on the left of the plate.

The water and juice glasses are placed on the right above the knife.

When serving, one should serve the dinner plate over the left shoulder of the guest and remove it from the right.

Try and use colour in the placemats, tablecloth, candles, and/or flowers to make the table cheerful and inviting.

Don't put pots and pans on the table. If you have young children in your family and don't want to clean up the mess of serving dishes, serve up the plates at the stove and bring the plates to the table.

Use dinner time to enjoy communicating the events of the day and try not to discipline children during mealtime.

Insist that children learn table manners at an early age. They will thank you later.

> *"Manners means treating others with respect,*
> *making them comfortable in your presence."*
> **- - Quin Sherrer, "A House of Many Blessings."**

This rule applies not only to guests, but to one another as a family. Remember, parents, that you are an important role model to your children and you can have a great influence on your children during the dinner hour.

Family prayers are also appropriate at mealtime. Let the children say grace and encourage them to include special needs that have arisen during the day.

My prayer for you is that you will be inspired to be creative in your meal preparation, serve one another joyfully and extend hospitality to those around you on a budget that you can afford.

Table of Contents

APPETIZERS

Concentrated Iced Tea Mix

10 tea bags

4 cups water

3 cups sugar

1 cup lemon juice

Boil water with tea bags and add the rest of the ingredients. Cool and add water and ice to taste.

Fruit Punch

3 cans frozen orange juice

2 cans frozen lemonade

1 litre pineapple juice

3 bananas mashed

1 litre of Ginger Ale or Sprite

berries (optional)

Mix together while partially frozen. Add a litre of Ginger Ale or Sprite and 5 juice cans of water. Put in punch bowl and add ice and any berries you choose.

Notes:

Bruschetta

1 loaf baguette, sliced thin on a diagonal

Olive oil

6 Roma tomatoes, chopped fine

2 Tbsp onions, chopped

2 cloves garlic, crushed

1/2 cup fresh basil chopped

2 tsp red wine vinegar

6 Tbsp olive oil

1/2 cup feta cheese, chopped

1 cup mozzarella cheese, shredded

Lightly brush slices of bread with olive oil. Broil until lightly browned.

Mix remaining ingredients except mozzarella cheese. Place vegetable mixture on toasted bread and sprinkle with the mozzarella cheese. Broil again until cheese is melted and golden brown.

Great as an appetizer or served with soup.

Notes:

Hot Crabmeat Cocktail Spread

Keep cocktail spread warm over a candle warmer. Serve with assorted crackers. Have spreaders handy.

1 (8 oz) pkg cream cheese

1 Tbsp milk

2 tsp Worcestershire sauce

6 oz crabmeat

2 Tbsp chopped green onions

2 Tbsp toasted slivered almonds

Thoroughly combine cream cheese, milk, and Worcestershire sauce. Drain and flake crabmeat. Add crabmeat and green onions to cheese mixture. Turn into a small shallow, greased baking dish. Bake in 350°F oven for 15 minutes or until heated through (or in microwave at medium heat).

Layered Taco Dip

1 lb lean ground beef

1 (4 oz) can chopped green chilies, undrained

2 tsp beef flavour instant bouillon

1 (15 oz or 16 oz) can refried beans

1 (16 oz) container sour cream

1 (1.7 oz) package taco seasoning mix

Guacamole (optional)

In large skillet, brown beef, pour off fat. Add chilies and bouillon. Cook and stir until bouillon dissolves. Cool. Stir in refried beans. In small bowl, combine sour cream and taco seasoning; set aside. In 7" or 8" spring-form pan or large plate, spread beef mixture. Top with sour cream mixture and guacamole. Cover. Chill several hours. Just before serving, remove side of spring form pan. Garnish with shredded cheese, chopped tomatoes, green onions, and olives. Serve with tortilla chips. Makes 12-15 servings.

Crab Spread

Serves 12

8 oz cream cheese

1/2 cup sour cream

1/4 cup mayonnaise

Mix together and spread on 12" decorative deep side plate or in a spring form pan.

Then layer on top of the spread:

1 cup crabmeat

1 cup cocktail sauce

2 cups shredded mozzarella cheese

1 chopped green pepper

3 green onions, chopped

1 tomato, diced

Serve with assorted crackers.

Notes:

SALADS

Bean Salad

I can green beans

I can wax beans

I can kidney beans

I medium size green pepper, chopped

I medium size white onion, chopped

1/4 cup salad oil

1/2 cup cider vinegar

I 1/2 tsp salt

1/2 tsp black pepper

Drain all beans well. Rinse kidney beans well. Combine all ingredients. Let marinate overnight. Best after 3 or 4 days. Use less oil if cutting down on fat. Serves 6-8,

N o t e s :

Greek Salad

1 head lettuce, cut up

1/2 - 1 small red onion, sliced thin

1/2 - 1 green pepper

1 cucumber, sliced

1/2 cup pitted black olives

1 cup finely chopped celery

1/2 – 3/4 carton (500 g) Feta cheese, crumbled

3 tomatoes cut in wedges

Can be prepared the day before and stored in the refrigerator in a plastic bag until just prior to serving.

DRESSING:

3/4 cup olive oil

1/2 cup white vinegar

2 Tbsp lemon juice

2 tsp sugar

Pepper and salt to taste

1/4 tsp garlic powder

3 tsp oregano

Shake and store, adding to salad just prior to serving.

Notes:

Sliced Cucumbers in Sour Cream and Dill

The tang and creaminess of cucumbers in this special dressing make for a pleasant change from the customary tossed salad. (No fat sour cream would make this a low fat recipe)

2 medium-size cucumbers

Salt

I cup sour cream

2 Tbsp vinegar

1/4 tsp sugar

1/8 tsp dried tarragon (optional)

1/2 tsp onion salt

I Tbsp minced fresh dill

Do not pare cucumbers. Slice very thin, sprinkle well with salt and allow to stand 10 minutes. Meanwhile, combine remaining ingredients. Pour off water that has accumulated around cucumbers and press slices dry between paper towels. Combine with dressing. Serve well chilled. Serves 6.

N o t e s :

Caesar Salad

DRESSING:

2 cloves garlic, crushed

1 egg yolk

2 fillets anchovies

8 Tbsp oil

1 Tbsp wine vinegar

Juice of 1/2 of a lemon

Dash of Worcestershire sauce

Dash of Tabasco sauce

Blend the above in the blender and mix the following:

1/2 cup green onions

2-3 oz Parmesan cheese

1 head of romaine lettuce, torn in pieces

Ground pepper

1 cup croutons

Pour dressing on lettuce mixture just before serving.

Notes:

Lettuce, Orange and Onion Salad

6 cups assorted salad greens

I large red Italian onion

3 large seedless oranges or 2 tins orange sections, drained

I/2 tsp salt

I/4 cup slivered almonds

DRESSING:

Freshly ground black pepper

5 Tbsp low-fat mayonnaise-type salad dressing

I Tbsp fresh orange juice or concentrated frozen

I Tbsp fresh lemon juice or bottled juice

I clove minced garlic

Alternate Dressing: *3/4 cup Miracle Whip, I clove garlic, I heaping tablespoon frozen orange juice from concentrate, 1/4 cup honey, salt and pepper. Put all ingredients in blender to liquefy.*

Wash and tear greens into bite size pieces. Arrange in a large salad bowl. Peel onions and oranges and slice both very thin. Sprinkle salt and pepper over greens, toss gently. Arrange alternate slices of onion and orange on top of greens. Mix dressing ingredients. Sprinkle dressing and slivered almonds over salad. Toss and serve. Serves 8.

Notes:

Crunchy Romaine Toss

Serves 10 – 12

1 cup walnuts or pecans, chopped

1 pkg Ramen Noodles, uncooked, broken up (discard the flavor packet)

4 Tbsp unsalted butter

1 bunch broccoli, coarsely chopped

1 head romaine lettuce, washed, broken into pieces

4 green onions, chopped

1 cup sweet and sour dressing (see below)

Brown walnuts and noodles in butter; cool on paper towels.
Combine noodles and walnuts with broccoli, romaine, and onions.

SWEET AND SOUR DRESSING

1/2 cup vegetable oil

1/2 cup sugar

1/4 cup wine vinegar

1 Tbsp soy sauce

Salt and pepper to taste

Blend and mix ingredients

Pour Sweet and Sour Dressing over and toss to coat well.

Notes:

Swedish Salad

3 pears, sliced

I cucumber, sliced

I red-skinned onion, sliced

DRESSING:

1/2 cup white vinegar

1/4 cup sugar

2 whole allspice

I tsp dill weed

I bay leaf

I tsp salt

Mix and let stand for at least 30 minutes to blend flavor. This salad is a great accompaniment to curried shrimp.

Lo-Cal Salad Dressing

This is a low calorie dressing given to me by Dr. Mary Ruth Swope:

I cup cottage cheese

1/4 cup chili sauce

2 Tbsp pickle relish

I Tbsp onion (chives)

Salt and pepper

Blend until smooth in the blender.

SOUPS

Miracle Soup - Low Cal

The miracle is that if you eat this for lunch every day you can lose weight. Of course, eat less for breakfast and dinner and pass up those fabulous desserts.

6 large onions

2 green peppers

2 large cans of tomatoes

1 large head cabbage, chopped

1 bunch celery, sliced

4 large carrots, sliced

2 pkgs dry onion soup mix

Cut vegetables, place in large pot, cover with water and bring to a boil. Add onion soup mix. Boil for 10 minutes, lower heat and cook until vegetables are soft. Add any spices you wish, e.g. chili, curry, bay leaf, thyme, or whole pepper. Serves 8-10.

N o t e s :

French Onion Soup

4-5 large yellow onions, sliced

3 Tbsp butter or margarine

1/4 tsp coarsely ground black pepper

1 Tbsp flour

3 cans beef broth, undiluted

3 cups water

1 bay leaf

Salt and pepper

6-8 slices French bread

2 Tbsp Parmesan cheese

1 cup grated Gruyere, Swiss, or Mozzarella cheese

1 Tbsp Worcestershire sauce

1/2 cup dry sherry or wine (optional)

Sauté onions in butter and pepper, stirring frequently until onions are light golden brown. Sprinkle onions with flour and stir until all traces of flour disappear. Cook 1 minute longer and then remove from heat. Gradually add beef broth. Return to moderately high heat and bring mixture to boil. Add bay leaf. Reduce heat to low and cook onion soup, uncovered for 30-40 minutes. Discard bay leaf. Turn soup into broiler-proof individual onion soup bowls and place on a jelly roll pan. Toast the French bread slices in a toaster or under the broiler until they are a light golden brown. Arrange toast slices on top of onion soup. Sprinkle toast liberally with the Parmesan and grated cheese. Place pan with broiler-proof bowls 6 inches under a preheated broiler until cheese melts and turns golden. Remove from oven and serve immediately. Serves 4-6.

Notes:

Minestrone Soup

1/2 cup olive oil

3 Tbsp butter

1 cup thinly sliced yellow onion

1 cup diced celery

1 cup carrots, diced

2 cups diced, peeled potatoes

1 1/2 cups fresh white beans, if available, or 1 1/2 cups canned canneline or kidney beans

2 cups diced zucchini

1 cup diced green beans

3 cups shredded cabbage

6 cups meat broth

1 19 oz can canned Italian tomatoes with their juice

PESTO:

3 cloves mashed garlic

6 Tbsp tomato paste or 9 Tbsp fresh tomato puree

2 Tbsp dried basil

3/4 cup combination of grated Parmesan and Romano cheese

(Use less oil, butter and Parmesan for healthy version.)

In oil and butter, cook onion over medium-low heat until onion wilts and turns pale gold, but is not browned. Add diced carrots and cook for 2 to 3 minutes, stirring occasionally. Repeat this procedure with the celery, potatoes, white beans, zucchini, and green beans; cooking each one a few minutes and stirring. Then add cabbage and cook for 6 minutes. Add the broth, the tomatoes in juice, and a little salt. Cover and cook at a very low boil for at least 3 hours. If necessary, you may stop the cooking at any time and resume later on. Minestrone should be cooked until thick like stew. Correct seasoning as required. Just before serving, mix pesto and add to soup. Mix well. Serves 6-8.

Chicken Corn Chowder

You can have this soup ready in less than 30 minutes.

2 Tbsp butter

1/4 cup chopped onion

1/4 cup chopped celery

2 Tbsp all-purpose flour

3 cups 2 % milk

2 cups chopped roasted skinless, boneless chicken breasts

(about 2 breast halves)

1 (14 3/4oz) can cream-style corn

1 1/2 cups fresh or frozen corn kernels (about 3 ears)

1 tsp chopped fresh or 1/4 tsp dried thyme

1/4 tsp cayenne pepper

1/8 tsp salt

Melt butter in a large Dutch Oven over medium heat. Add onion and celery and cook 3 minutes or until tender, stirring frequently. Add flour; cook 1 minute, stirring constantly. Stir in milk and remaining ingredients. Bring to a boil; cook until thick (about 5 minutes). Yield: 6 servings (serving size: about 1 cup).

N o t e s :

Chunky Potato - Crab Chowder

2 Tbsp butter

I cup chopped onion

3/4 cup chopped celery

I garlic clove, minced

3 1/2 cups 1"cubed red potato (about 1 lb)

3 Tbsp all-purpose flour

2 1/2 cups 2% milk

1/2 tsp dried thyme

1/2 tsp freshly ground black pepper

1/4 tsp grated whole nutmeg

I 14 3/4 oz can cream-style corn

I 14 oz can fat-free, less-sodium chicken broth

2 6-oz cans crabmeat

3 Tbsp chopped fresh parsley

I tsp salt

Sauté onion, celery and garlic until transparent. Add potato cubes, chicken broth and herbs. Cook until potatoes are tender. Mix milk with the flour, and then add to the soup, and then add the corn and cook until mixture is thick. Add drained crab and heat until bubbly, ladle into soup bowls and garnish with parsley.

N o t e s :

VEGETABLE

Potato Cheese Casserole

This recipe is very good with Ham or Roast Beef.

1 cup sour cream

1 can cream of mushroom soup

2 Tbsp melted butter

1 Tbsp finely chopped onion

1/2 tsp salt

1 cup grated medium cheddar cheese

4 cups frozen hashed brown potatoes

1/4 cup Parmesan cheese

In a large bowl, combine sour cream, mushroom soup, melted butter, chopped onion, salt, and cheddar cheese. Fold in frozen potatoes. Place in greased 9"x 9" baking dish. Sprinkle with Parmesan cheese. Bake at 325°F for 1 to 1 1/2 hours. Serves 4-6.

Easy Cheesy Scalloped Potatoes

1 can cheddar cheese soup

3/4 cup milk, heated

4 medium potatoes, peeled and sliced

1 onion, thinly sliced

Pepper

Paprika

In small bowl, combine soup and milk; blend together until smooth. Spoon one third of this mixture into bottom of a greased 1 1/2 quart covered casserole. Alternate layers of potato and onion slices, sprinkling each layer with pepper. Spoon remaining soup mixture over the top potato layer. Sprinkle with paprika. Cover and bake in oven at 350°F for 60 minutes or until potato slices are tender. Serves 4.

Potato Salad

8 potatoes (boiled whole unpeeled)

6-8 eggs, hard boiled

6 green onions, cut up

2 or 3 finely chopped pickles (optional)

DRESSING:

1/2 cup mayonnaise

1/2 cup milk or cream

1/4 cup vinegar

1 tsp salt

2 Tbsp sugar

1 tsp pepper

1/2 tsp dry mustard (to taste)

Peel and dice potatoes; peel and dice eggs. Mix the dressing and add to all of the above.

Notes:

Creamed Beets

(This is very good served with pork.)

**1 (1-lb) can sliced or diced beets
(approximately 2 cups)**

4 Tbsp sour cream

1 Tbsp vinegar

1 tsp sugar

1/2 tsp salt

1/8 tsp garlic powder

1/8 tsp onion powder

2 tsp minced fresh chives

Drain beets well and place in saucepan. Add remaining ingredients with the exception of the minced chives. Stir and heat through gently but thoroughly. Serve piping hot sprinkled with the minced fresh chives. Serves 4-5.

Green Bean Casserole

3 cans green beans or 1-2 lb frozen beans, cooked

1 pkg oriental vegetables or 1 pkg frozen corn - cooked

1 cup sour cream

1 can cream of celery soup

1 can cream of onion soup

1 small onion, chopped

1 cup shredded cheddar cheese

1 cup bread crumbs or herb stuffing

Slivered almonds

Combine sour cream, soup, onion and cheese. Add to vegetables. Top with crumbs or herb stuffing and almonds. Bake at 350°F for 45 minutes. Serves 8.

Broccoli with Lemon Mayonnaise - Low Cal

Lemon mayonnaise is the simplest of dressings for broccoli and is equally good on hot asparagus. The lemon mayonnaise itself does not require heating.

2 lbs. fresh broccoli or 2 pkgs. frozen broccoli

Cook just until tender in boiling, salted water.

LEMON MAYONNAISE:

1/2 cup mayonnaise (low or no fat)
2 Tbsp lemon juice
1/4 tsp Worcestershire sauce
1/8 tsp dry mustard
Pinch cayenne pepper

Combine ingredients thoroughly. Spoon on two or three wide ribbon-like bands across cooked, well-drained stalks of broccoli arranged in an oblong serving dish. Sprinkle lemon mayonnaise with paprika and serve at once. Serves 6.

Notes:

Zucchini Parmesan

2 lbs zucchini

2 Tbsp olive oil

I Tbsp butter

Salt

Pepper, freshly ground

Oregano

I bay leaf

3-4 Tbsp Parmesan cheese

Butter

Wash the zucchini, but do not peel. Slice into 1/4 inch discs and fry in a sizzling mixture of olive oil and butter. Turn the zucchini slices when golden brown. Sprinkle with salt, freshly ground black pepper, and a little oregano. Add a bay leaf, cover the skillet, and simmer for 5 minutes or until the zucchini is tender. Transfer to a shallow baking dish, preferably one that can be brought to the table. Sprinkle top thickly with Parmesan cheese, and dot with butter. Place beneath moderate broiler flame until cheese is lightly browned. Serve at once. Serves 6.

Panned Chinese Cabbage - Lo Cal

3 Tbsp olive oil

2 Tbsp slivered almonds, unblanched

I small head cabbage, shredded

I Tbsp Soya sauce

1/8 tsp freshly ground black pepper

Heat 1 Tbsp of the olive oil in a large skillet. Sauté slivered almonds until lightly browned, remove and drain on paper toweling. Add remaining oil and cabbage to the skillet, sprinkle with Soya sauce and pepper, cover skillet tightly, and steam for 7 or 8 minutes. Cabbage should be tender, but still crisp. Taste for seasoning, adding additional Soya sauce if necessary. Sprinkle with slivered almonds and serve at once. Serves 4-5.

Orange-Glazed Sweet Potatoes

1 – 14 oz can sweet potatoes

3 Tbsp butter or margarine

1/2 cup orange marmalade

1/2 tsp cinnamon

1/8 tsp nutmeg

1 Tbsp brandy or Cointreau (optional)

Drain sweet potatoes and slice in halves, or if very large, in quarters. Melt butter in a large skillet; add marmalade, cinnamon, nutmeg, and brandy. Cook until bubbling. Lay in sweet potatoes. Simmer uncovered, spooning marmalade mixture over and around them, and basting them from time to time until well glazed. This should take about 15 minutes. Serve sweet potatoes very hot with pan glaze spooned over them. If desired, potatoes and glaze may be dusted with cinnamon and run under the broiler flame for a few minutes before serving. Serves 4.

Corn Sauté

4 cobs of corn (or 3 cups frozen corn)

2 Tbsp butter

3 whole green onions, sliced

1 small red pepper, cored, seeded and finely diced

1/3 cup whipping cream or 3 Tbsp water

Dash of Tabasco sauce

Salt and pepper

Using a very sharp knife, slice corn kernels off cobs. They should measure about 3 cups. Set aside. Melt butter in a large, wide frying pan over medium heat. Add green onions and red pepper. Sauté for 2 minutes. Then add corn, cream or water, and Tabasco. Continue to cook, stirring frequently, over medium-low heat until corn is tender, about 5 to 6 minutes. Taste and add salt and pepper as needed. Serves 6.

Creamed Onions

Very Good

12 medium onions, peeled

4 Tbsp butter

4 Tbsp flour

2 cups milk

I tsp salt

Grated Parmesan cheese

Paprika

Cut onions in half. Cover with water and boil gently just until tender. Drain. Arrange cut-side down in buttered 9" shallow baking dish. Melt butter in saucepan. Remove from heat and blend in flour. Gradually stir in milk. Add salt. Cook over medium heat, stirring constantly until thickened. Pour sauce over onions. Sprinkle Parmesan cheese generously over top; then sprinkle with paprika. Bake in 350°F oven for 20 minutes. If creamed onions have been made ahead of time, heat through in 325°F oven for about 30 minutes. Very good with Roast Beef or Turkey. Serves 6.

Notes:

Creamed Brussels Sprouts

A vegetable dish of such elegance and delicacy that it may be served with pride along with a fine, juicy prime rib of beef at a company dinner. Yet it is simple enough to prepare so that the family, too, may enjoy its wonderful texture and flavor. Best with plain broiled meats—either chops or steaks—or with roast. Preparation time: 30 minutes.

1 can sliced chestnuts or 1/2 cup toasted almonds

1 package frozen Brussels sprouts

2 Tbsp butter

2 Tbsp flour

3/4 cup light cream

1/2 tsp salt

1/8 white pepper

1/8 tsp nutmeg

Cook Brussels sprouts according to directions on the package. Drain the freshly cooked Brussels sprouts, removing them from the saucepan in which they were cooked. Melt the butter in the same saucepan, stir in flour, and blend smooth, holding the saucepan off the heat as you do this. Add the milk or cream a little at a time. Heat gently, stirring until thickened. Add the salt, white pepper, and nutmeg, then the Brussels sprouts and the nuts. Stir gently, being careful not to tear the leaves off the cooked sprouts. Taste for seasoning. Serve very hot in a warm vegetable dish. A little additional nutmeg may be added. Serves 4-5.

Notes:

Peas with Mushrooms

2 Tbsp butter

2 (10 oz) pkgs frozen green peas,

thawed just enough to be broken into small chunks

1 small onion, sliced in half

Large lettuce leaves

3 Tbsp butter

1/4 lb mushrooms, sliced

1 Tbsp minced fresh parsley

1/8 tsp marjoram

Salt

Pepper

In heavy saucepan, melt the 2 Tbsp of butter and add the frozen green peas in chunks and the onion halves. Cover peas with large lettuce leaves, tucking leaves in well around the peas. Cover saucepan and simmer gently for 15-20 minutes or until peas are tender. Add no water during cooking process. Melt 3 Tbsp of butter in a skillet. Add the sliced mushrooms, and sauté until tender. Combine with the cooked peas (discarding lettuce leaves and onion) and add the parsley, marjoram, salt and pepper to taste. Heat thoroughly and serve. Serves 8.

N o t e s :

Sweet and Sour Green Beans

Very Good!

2 lbs fresh or frozen green beans

1 cup water

2 slices bacon

1/2 cup diced onion

1 Tbsp all-purpose flour

1/4 cup white vinegar

2 Tbsp sugar

1 tsp salt

1/4 tsp pepper

Wash beans; trim ends, and remove strings. Bring water to a boil in a Dutch oven. Add beans. Cover and cook 10 minutes or until crisp-tender. Drain beans, reserving 3/4 cup liquid. Set beans and liquid aside.

Cook bacon in a large skillet until crisp; remove bacon, reserving drippings in skillet. Crumble bacon and set aside. Sauté onion in skillet until tender. Add flour. Cook 1 minute, stirring constantly. Add green beans; toss to coat. Cover and heat thoroughly. Spoon into serving bowl and sprinkle with crumbled bacon. Yield: 8 servings.

Notes:

RICE

Risotto

1 cup Arborio rice

2 Tbsp olive oil

1 large onion, peeled and finely diced

1/2 cup dry white wine

1 1/2 cups chicken stock

2 Tbsp unsalted butter

1/4 cup freshly grated parmesan cheese

2 Tbsp whipping cream

Using a large skillet with a heavy bottom, heat the olive oil over low heat and sauté or "sweat" the onions until translucent, being careful not to allow them to colour or brown. Add the Arborio rice, stir to coat with the olive oil, and sauté with the onions to toast each grain of rice, about 7 minutes. This toasting process adds the chewy, al dente quality that is attractive about risotto.

Once rice is lightly toasted, add white wine slowly, stirring with a wooden spoon (a metal one tends to injure the rice). Constant stirring should also be avoided.

Preheat the chicken stock just to boiling and have it ready beside the stove. After the rice has absorbed the white wine and the skillet is nearly dry, add one cup of chicken stock while stirring occasionally. Continue cooking over low heat until all the chicken stock is absorbed by the rice. Adding the liquid in stages rather than all at once allows the rice to expand more fully, adding to the creamy texture of risotto. This cooking process will take about 20 minutes.

After all the liquid has been added and the rice is still chewy, but fully cooked, add the butter, Parmesan cheese and heavy cream. Stir to combine everything and serve immediately.

PASTA

Lasagna

SAUCE:

2 lb minced meat

3 cans (15 oz) tomato sauce

1/2 cup green pepper, diced

1 tsp garlic powder or 1 clove garlic

1 tsp oregano

2 Tbsp minced onion

2 tsp sugar

1 tsp rosemary

Sauté meat, drain fat; add the remaining ingredients, and bring to a boil. Simmer for 30 minutes.

CHEESE MIXTURE:

2 pints cottage cheese (un-creamed)

4 tsp salt

2 Tbsp parsley flakes

2 eggs

1/4 tsp pepper

1 cup grated Parmesan cheese

Mix the above ingredients together.

1 pkg lasagna noodles, boiled until al dente

1 lb mozzarella cheese – thinly sliced

In 9"x 13" pan or lasagna casserole, layer in order: 1/2 noodles, 1/2 cottage cheese, 1/2 meat. Repeat with remaining ingredients. Sprinkle with mozzarella cheese. Bake at 350°F for 30-45 minutes. Serves 6.

Fettuccini with Ham

1/3 lb fettuccini or egg noodles

1/4 cup butter

3 cloves garlic, minced

1/2 cup finely chopped green onions

1 1/2 cups diced cooked ham or browned bacon

1/2 cup milk

1 egg, lightly beaten

3/4 cup grated Parmesan cheese

Dash Worcestershire sauce

Salt and freshly ground pepper

In large pot of boiling, salted water, cook noodles until al dente (tender, but firm) or according to package directions. Drain and return pasta to pot.

In skillet, melt butter over medium heat. Cook garlic and onions for 2-3 minutes or until tender; stir in ham. Add to hot noodles along with milk, egg and cheese. Toss well. Add Worcestershire sauce and salt and pepper to taste; toss again. Serve immediately. Serves 3-4.

Notes:

Fettuccini Alfredo

1/2 of a 900 g package Fettuccini
1/3 cup butter, softened
3/4 cup whipping cream, room temperature, divided
3/4 cup Parmesan cheese
1/8 tsp white pepper
Pinch ground nutmeg
Coarsely ground pepper
Grated Parmesan cheese
1 clove garlic, chopped (or 1/2 tsp garlic powder)

In large heavy saucepan, cook Fettuccini just until tender; drain. In same pan, (remove from heat) combine hot fettuccini and butter; toss to coat. Add 1/2 of the cream; toss well. Add remaining cream; toss well. Add remaining Parmesan cheese, white pepper and nutmeg; toss well with 2 forks until fettuccini is coated and sauce is creamy. Arrange in warm serving dish. Serve immediately with pepper and Parmesan cheese. Makes 4-6 servings.

TIPS FOR PERFECT FETTUCCINI ALFREDO

Take hot saucepan off stove top while adding remaining ingredients to fettuccini or the butter will separate and the sauce will not be creamy.

The fettuccini and the saucepan must be hot when other ingredients are added. Since the saucepan is not on the burner, the heat from the fettuccini is needed to melt the butter and Parmesan cheese to form a creamy sauce.

Toss fettuccini gently with two long-handled plastic forks to separate and coat the fettuccini without breaking it.

Fettuccini must be tossed very well to allow pasta to absorb the cream and yield a creamy sauce.

Place fettuccini in warm serving bowl to help keep it hot and serve immediately.

Enjoy this dish as soon as it is ready because it does not hold or reheat well.

Three Cheese Noodle Casserole

This delicious main dish can be made the day before and refrigerated until needed.

1 (8 oz) package ruffled egg noodles

1 cup sour cream

6 oz cream cheese, softened

1/2 cup finely chopped onion

1 minced garlic clove

1 1/2 pounds lean ground beef

1 (15 oz) can tomato sauce with tomato pieces

1 tsp oregano

1/4 cup Parmesan cheese

1/4 tsp salt

Pepper to taste

Shredded cheddar cheese

Cook noodles according to package directions. Drain. Beat sour cream and cream cheese together. Stir in onions and the garlic and set aside. Brown the ground beef in a skillet, crumbling it with a fork as it cooks. Stir in tomato sauce, oregano, Parmesan cheese, salt and pepper. Simmer 10 minutes. In a 2-quart baking dish, layer half the noodles, half the sour cream mixture, and half the beef mixture. Repeat layers, ending with the beef mixture, and top with shredded cheese. Cover tightly with plastic wrap. Refrigerate overnight. Bake 30 minutes or until heated through. Let stand 5 minutes before serving. Serves 6.

Notes:

Spaghetti Sauce

1 long pepperoni stick, sliced fine

1/2 lb ground beef

1 large onion, diced

1 tsp garlic powder or 2-3 cloves of garlic

1 tsp salt

1 tsp pepper

1 tsp Accent

2 tins mushrooms, stems and pieces

48 oz tin of tomato juice

2 (8 oz) tins tomato paste

4 whole bay leaves

1/2 cup fresh parsley, chopped

1 tsp oregano

2 tsp chili powder or more

1/2 cup water

In large pot, brown pepperoni, ground beef, and onion. Add remaining ingredients, including meat balls (recipe next page). Sauce should simmer all day on top of stove.

This sauce can also be served with chicken.

Notes:

Spaghetti Meatballs

3 pounds of ground beef

1 cup grated cheese

4 eggs, beaten

1 cup bread crumbs

1/2 cup water

2 tsp salt

1/2 tsp pepper

1 tsp garlic powder

1/4 cup chives

In small bowl, beat 4 eggs. In second bowl, combine bread crumbs and water. In large bowl combine ground beef, cheese, beaten eggs, and spices with bread crumbs and water mixture. Mix well. Shape into balls and place on oiled broiler pan. Bake at 350°F for 15-20 minutes. Remove meatballs from pan, draining well, and add to sauce. Serve on cooked spaghetti. Serves 8.

Macaroni Casserole – Quick & Easy

2 cups uncooked macaroni

1 lb ground beef

1 onion, chopped

1 tsp salt

Pepper

1 can mushroom soup

1 can tomato soup

Cook and drain macaroni. Brown beef and onions. Drain. Add seasoning and undiluted soups. Mix with macaroni and put into casserole dish. Bake at 350°F for 30 minutes.

Sambucca and Shrimp Pasta

Frozen or fresh ravioli is also a
good substitute for the fettuccine

1 lb of frozen cooked shrimp

3 Tbsp Sambucca

1/2 onion diced

1 garlic crushed

1/2 red pepper finely diced

1/2 green pepper finely diced

1/2 lb mushrooms finely sliced

3/4 cup hot water with 1 chicken boullion

1/2 cup chopped parsley

3/4 cup whipping cream

1/4 cup Parmesan cheese

12 oz fettuccine noodles

Salt

Pepper

Thaw the shrimp, drain and marinade with Sambucca. Cook pasta as directed on package – al dente. Melt the butter in frying pan; add onion, mushroom, garlic, and red and green peppers. Add the hot water bullion, the whipping cream and salt and pepper to taste. Simmer until syrupy. Add the shrimp and Sambucca just long enough to heat. Do not overcook.

Pour mixture over the pasta on each plate and sprinkle with Parmesan and parsley. Serves 4-6.

Pasta with Pepper

*Excellent dish - really good with shish kabob chicken
and Chicken Roquefort.*

2 Tbsp butter or margarine, melted

3 Tbsp olive oil

3 cloves garlic, minced

I tsp grated lemon rind

1/4 tsp crushed red pepper

I – (14 1/2 oz) can ready-to-serve chicken broth

3 Tbsp lemon juice

1/2 tsp salt

1/2 tsp freshly ground pepper

16 oz uncooked fettuccini

2 sweet red peppers cut into strips

Heat butter and oil in a medium saucepan. Add garlic, lemon rind, and crushed red pepper, and cook over low heat 2 minutes, stirring occasionally. Add chicken broth and lemon juice, and simmer over medium heat until reduced to about 1 1/4 cups (about 25 minutes). Add salt and pepper.

Cook fettuccini in large Dutch Oven according to package directions. Drain. Return fettuccini to Dutch oven; add red pepper strips and broth mixture. Cook over low heat I minute or until thoroughly heated, tossing gently. Serve immediately, or if desired, spoon into a lightly greased 13"x 9"x 2" baking dish. Cover and chill. Remove from refrigerator and let stand at room temperature I hour. Bake, covered at 350°F for 30 minutes. Yield: 8 servings.

BREAKFAST

&

BRUNCH

Pancakes - Willard's Famous Recipe

SINGLE BATCH:

2 cups flour

1 tsp salt

1 tsp baking soda

1 1/2 tsp baking powder

2 tsp sugar

Mix dry ingredients together first, and add the following:

2 cups buttermilk or regular milk with 1/4 cup vinegar

2 eggs

2 Tbsp cooking oil

Mix wet ingredients together in blender. Add wet ingredients to dry. Preheat griddle to 400°F and pour a ladle full for each pancake. When the batter bubbles, turn over on other side. Unless you use a frying pan that sticks do NOT use oil or butter to grease the grill. Serve with maple or fruit syrup and plenty of bacon or sausages. Serves 3-4.

Notes:

Waffles

1 3/4 cup flour

1 tsp salt

1 Tbsp sugar

4 tsp baking powder

2 eggs, separated

1/4 cup vegetable oil

1 3/4 cup milk

Mix dry ingredients. Mix egg yolks, oil and milk and add to the dry mix. Beat egg whites and fold into batter. Serves 2

Serve with maple syrup or fresh syrup, or the following sweet vanilla sauce:

Sweet Vanilla Sauce

Fabulous topping for waffles.

2 cups milk

1/4 cup sugar

3/4 cup of waffle batter (above)

1 tsp vanilla

1 Tbsp butter

Beat ingredients together. Heat in microwave, mixing often until thick and bubbly. Add 1 tsp vanilla and 1 Tbsp butter and serve on top of waffles.

Add fresh fruit and/or maple syrup to taste.

Quiche Lorraine

One – 8" pastry shell. Bake 5 minutes at 425°F.

3-4 oz lean bacon, partially fried, cut in small pieces

2 or 3 eggs

1/2 tsp salt

1 1/2 - 2 cups whipping cream

Pinch of pepper and nutmeg

3/4 cup grated Swiss cheese

Mix cream, eggs, and salt in blender for about 30 seconds. Stir in pepper and nutmeg. Place bacon on bottom of pastry shell with 1/2 cup grated cheese. Pour in liquid and sprinkle rest of Swiss cheese on the top. Bake at 350°F for 25-30 minutes or until quiche has puffed. Serves 4-6.

Quick & Easy Tasty Quiche

1 cup sharp cheddar cheese, grated

1 cup half'n half (or milk or water)

1/4 cup BisQuick

3 or 4 eggs

Using a 10" pie plate, put in broccoli, mushrooms, spinach, onion, green pepper, ham, crumbled bacon, and whatever else you like for a filling. Put the cheese on top of the filling. Blend in the remaining ingredients. Pour into a pie plate. Bake at 350 °F for 30 minutes and then cool for 10 minutes. Serves 6.

Notes:

Baked Apple Pancake

6 eggs

1 1/2 cups milk

1 cup flour

3 Tbsp white sugar

1 tsp vanilla

1/2 tsp salt

1/4 tsp cinnamon

1/4 lb butter or margarine

2 apples, peeled and thinly sliced

2-3 Tbsp brown sugar

Preheat oven to 425°F. In a blender or large bowl mix eggs, milk, flour, sugar, vanilla, salt, and cinnamon until well blended. Melt butter or margarine in a 12" fluted porcelain quiche dish or 13"x 9" baking dish in oven. Swirl to distribute melted butter evenly over bottom of pan. Add apples to baking dish. Return to oven until butter sizzles. Do not let brown. Remove dish from oven and immediately pour batter over apples. Sprinkle with brown sugar and a little additional cinnamon if you like. Bake in the middle of the oven 20 minutes or until puffed and golden brown. Serve immediately. Serves 3-4.

Make sure you have a jug of maple syrup and/or a bowl of freshly whipped cream to compliment the pancake.

Notes :

Crepes

(For Blintzes or German Pancakes)

BATTER:
3 eggs

1 1/4 cup flour

1/4 tsp salt

1 cup milk

1/2 cup water

Butter

Blend eggs, milk and water. Add flour and salt and stir until smooth. If batter is too thin to handle, add a little flour. Let stand for at least 15 minutes. In level-bottom skillet, melt 1/4 tsp butter; spread evenly over skillet. When butter begins to sizzle, pour enough batter in the pan to coat the bottom, (f using as crepe or pancake). When batter is dry, flip over and brown the other side.

For Blintzes, cook only the one side and invert onto a dry tea towel until cool. Put filling on the brown side of the blintz. Fold over like an envelope. Put butter on bottom of the pan, and fry the blintz on both sides.

FRESH BLUEBERRY TOPPING:
2 cups fresh blueberries

1/2 cup water

1/4 cup sugar

1 Tbsp cornstarch

1 tsp lemon juice

Wash and sort blueberries. Combine in saucepan with the water and cook over a very low heat for 5 minutes until blueberries are tender, but still plump and whole. Drain berries, reserving 1/4 cup of the juice. Combine sugar and cornstarch in saucepan. Add reserved 1/4 cup of blueberry liquid and lemon juice. Blend until smooth and cook, stirring until mixture becomes very thick. Cool slightly and add the blueberries.

Crepes...continued

CHERRY TOPPING:

These cherry blintzes are delicious served sizzling hot with cold sour cream. Prepare crepes exactly as for blueberry blintzes.

1 (1 lb) can pitted red sour cherries, water pack

2 Tbsp cornstarch

2/3 cup sugar

1/2 tsp almond extract

Drain cherries, reserving juice, and measure off 2/3 cup. Combine cornstarch and sugar in a saucepan, blending well. Add cherry juice, a little at a time, mix smooth and cook, stirring until mixture becomes glossy and very thick. Cook slightly, add almond extract and drained cherries. Mix thoroughly, taste for flavor and cool.

CHEESE FILLING:

1/4 lb small-curd cottage cheese

1/4 lb cream cheese

2 egg yolks

4 Tbsp sugar

1/2 tsp salt

1/2 tsp cinnamon

2 tsp grated lemon rind

3 Tbsp raisins (optional)

Combine cheeses and blend thoroughly. Beat in egg yolks and add remaining ingredients. Taste for flavor. Due to the firmer nature of the filling, these cheese blintzes may be folded somewhat differently from the fruit-filled blintzes. Distribute the filling evenly among 10-12 crepes, placing the cheese in the center of each crepe. Lap edge nearest you over cheese to cover filling. Then lap sides over this. Lastly, flip blintz over onto far edge of crepe. This should produce a neat squarish or rectangular package. Fry as for fruit-filled blintzes. Cheese blintzes are most delicious served very hot with cold sour cream and cherry or blueberry topping.

Brunch Casserole

16 slices bread with crusts removed

6 eggs

1/2 tsp salt

1/2 tsp pepper

1/2 – 1 tsp dry mustard

1/4 cup minced onion

1/4 cup green peppers

1 - 2 tsp Worcestershire sauce

3 cups whole milk

1/4 lb butter

1/2 lb cheddar cheese

1/2 lb back bacon or diced ham

Crushed corn flakes

Put out 8 pieces of bread to cover a dish entirely, or use a 9"x 13" baking pan. Cover bread with slices of back bacon, lay thin slices of cheddar cheese on top of bacon, and then cover with slices of bread to make it like a sandwich. In a bowl beat eggs, salt pepper, and green pepper. Add mustard, onion, Worcestershire sauce, and milk. Pour over bread layers and let stand in refrigerator overnight. In morning melt 1/4 lb butter and add crushed flakes; put on top of casserole. Bake at 350°F for about 1 hour. Let stand 10 minutes before serving. Serves 8.

Notes:

MAIN DISHES

Turkey Pot Pie

1/3 cup butter

1/2 lb mushrooms

1/4 cup flour

1 cup chicken stock

2 cups milk

1/2 tsp thyme

1/4 tsp Tabasco sauce

1 tsp salt

4 cups diced turkey

1/4 cup pimento

1 pkg or 2 1/2 cups peas and carrots

In skillet, melt butter and sauté mushrooms. Add flour, stock, and milk. Cook until thickened and add seasoning, turkey, and vegetables. Simmer for 10 minutes. Place in deep casserole dish and cover with Biscuit Crust..

BISCUIT CRUST:

2 cups flour

4 tsp baking powder

2 Tbsp fresh dill

2 Tbsp fresh parsley

1/2 tsp salt

2/3 cup butter

1 cup milk

Combine flour, baking powder, dill, parsley, and salt. Cut in butter and add milk, kneading until well mixed. Roll out biscuit crust to make top crust for 9 inch casserole dish. Bake at 400°F for 30-35 minutes. Double the biscuit crust recipe for extra biscuits. Serves 6-8.

Chicken Creole Jambalaya - Low Fat

A wonderful way to use leftover chicken. For low-fat version, omit bacon.

3 cups chicken, sliced

3 slices of bacon, diced

1 clove garlic

2 large onions

1 Tbsp parsley

3 stalks celery

1 large green pepper

1 Tbsp flour

2 cups canned tomatoes

1 tsp sweet basil

1 1/2 tsp chili powder

1 1/2 tsp salt

1 tsp sugar

1/2 tsp Worcestershire sauce

Dash cayenne pepper

Cook diced bacon in skillet and add garlic, onion, celery, parsley and green pepper. Stir in flour and let sit a moment. Add tomatoes, basil, sugar, Worcestershire sauce and spices. Add water if necessary. Add the chicken and simmer for 20 minutes. Serve hot over cooked rice.

N o t e s :

Chicken A La King - Quick & Easy

2 Tbsp butter

1/4 lb fresh mushrooms

1/2 green pepper, cut fine

2 Tbsp butter

3 Tbsp flour

1/2 tsp salt

1/4 tsp paprika

1 cup rich milk or cereal cream

1 cup chicken stock

2 egg yolks

1 tsp lemon juice

3 cups cooked chicken, diced

Melt butter in a frying pan. Add mushrooms and pepper. Cook until fairly dry. In a saucepan, make a sauce of butter, flour, seasonings, milk and stock. Add egg yolks (well beaten) and lemon juice. Cook a moment; add mushrooms, green pepper, and chicken. Heat thoroughly. Serve on toast or pastry shells with tossed salad. Serves 4-6.

Chinese Baked Chicken - Quick & Easy

3 pieces chicken

1 Tbsp Soya sauce

Accent

2 Tbsp lemon juice

Lowry's seasoned salt

Lowry's seasoned pepper

Put chicken pieces in a casserole dish. Sprinkle with the rest of the ingredients, cover and bake at 400°F until chicken is done, 30 minutes. Serve with rice. Serves 2-3.

Chicken Supreme

Great easy dish for company — serve with rice.

4 boneless, skinless chicken breasts or legs

1/2 tsp lemon juice

1/4 tsp salt

Sprinkle lemon juice and salt on chicken breasts. Bake in oven for about 30 minutes at 350°F.

SAUCE:

4 Tbsp butter

1/4 lb mushrooms

1 Tbsp green onion

Sauté together and add:

1/4 cup beef bouillon

1/4 cup vermouth

1 cup whipping cream

2 Tbsp parsley

Boil to reduce the liquids until thick like syrup. Pour on chicken and bake another 15 minutes.

Notes:

Roquefort Chicken

1 cup fresh sourdough breadcrumbs (or regular)

1 (1 1/2) oz can grated parmesan cheese

1/4 tsp salt

1/4 tsp freshly ground pepper

1 1/4 tsp dried whole thyme

3 Tbsp butter or margarine, melted

3 Tbsp olive oil

1/4 cup milk

1 Tbsp white wine

Worcestershire sauce

8 chicken breast halves, skinned and de-boned

Roquefort Sauce (next page)

Crumbled Roquefort cheese, (optional)

Fresh thyme, (optional)

Combine first 5 ingredients in a pie-plate. Combine butter, oil, milk, wine and Worcestershire sauce. Dip each chicken breast in milk mixture and dredge in crumb mixture. Arrange chicken in a lightly greased 15" x 10" x 1" jelly roll pan. Bake at 350°F for 30-35 minutes or until tender. Serve with Roquefort Sauce drizzled over chicken. If desired, garnish with crumbled cheese and fresh thyme. Yield: 8 servings.

Notes:

Roquefort Chicken...continued

ROQUEFORT SAUCE:

1 shallot, chopped

1 stalk celery with leaves, chopped

2 Tbsp butter or margarine, melted

1/2 cup white wine

1 (10 3/4 oz) can condensed chicken broth, undiluted

1 cup whipping cream

2 Tbsp crumbled Roquefort or blue cheese

1 Tbsp chopped fresh chives

Sauté shallot and celery in butter in a medium saucepan until tender. Add wine and chicken broth. Bring to a boil and cook over medium heat, stirring frequently until liquid is reduced to about 1 cup (about 15 minutes). Strain. Return broth mixture to saucepan. Add whipping cream and return to a boil. Reduce heat and simmer about 15 minutes or until mixture is reduced to about 1 cup, stirring frequently. Remove from heat. Add cheese and stir until cheese melts. Stir in chopped chives. Serve with pasta.

Notes:

Shish Kebob Chicken Barbeque

4 chicken breast halves, skinned and de-boned

SAUCE:

1 cup salsa

2 Tbsp vegetable oil

1 Tbsp lime juice

2 cloves garlic, minced

1/2 tsp ground cumin

1/2 tsp dried whole oregano, crushed

1/4 tsp salt

Additional salsa

Place each chicken breast between 2 pieces of plastic wrap. Flatten chicken to 1/4" thickness using a meat mallet or rolling pin. Cut into 1" wide strips. Place in a shallow container. Pour sauce over chicken. Cover and chill 1-2 hours.

Thread chicken onto skewers. I add cherry tomatoes, green peppers, mushrooms and onion. Cook over hot coals 6-8 minutes or until done, turning occasionally and basting with remaining marinade. Serve with picanté sauce. Yield: 4 servings.

Notes :

Chicken Marinade

...for the barbeque

1 cup oil

2 cups vinegar

3 Tbsp salt

1 Tbsp poultry seasoning

1 tsp pepper

1 egg

Beat egg. Add oil. Beat again. Add other ingredients. Mix well. Marinate chicken pieces in this marinade for several hours. Then barbeque the chicken.

Apricot Roast Pork - Low Fat

3 lb boneless pork-loin roast

1/2 cup apricot jam

2 Tbsp chili sauce

1 Tbsp red-wine vinegar

1 Tbsp Dijon mustard

Preheat oven to 325°F. Lightly oil a shallow roasting pan. Place roast in pan, fat-side up.

In a small bowl, stir apricot jam with remaining ingredients. If there are any large pieces of apricot in the jam, remove and finely chop, and then stir into mixture.

Smear sauce all over roast. If using a meat thermometer, insert in center of roast. Roast pork in oven, uncovered, basting occasionally for about 1 1/2 hours or 30 minutes per pound, until internal temperature reaches 160°F. Baste occasionally. Let sit for 10 minutes before carving.

Rice and Curry - Quick & Easy

Cook 2- 2 1/2 cups of rice according to directions.

2 lbs ground beef (or leftover chicken or beef)

1 (28 oz) can tomatoes

1 small onion, chopped

1 Tbsp curry powder – to taste

1/4 cup sugar

2 tsp salt

Add pepper and Tabasco to taste

Leftover gravy if available (approximately 1 cup)

1/4 cup whipping cream

In frying pan, brown ground beef and onion. Drain the fat. Add curry powder, sugar, salt, and pepper. Add tomatoes and simmer for about 10-15 minutes. Taste for seasoning. You might like more curry and Tabasco sauce. Just before serving add whipping cream. This is a very quick & easy supper meal. Serve with rice and condiments like bananas, peanuts, shredded coconuts, etc. Serves 4-6.

Notes :

Meatloaf Wellington

Elegance plus economy.

2 lbs lean ground beef

2 eggs

1/4 tsp pepper

1 cup of bread crumbs

2 tsp Worcestershire sauce

1 pkg dehydrated onion soup mix

2/3 cup milk

1/8 tsp garlic powder

1/4 cup finely chopped pimento

1/3 cup finely chopped green pepper

Pastry for a two-crust pie or puff pastry

1 egg for glaze

Combine all ingredients except the pie crust and egg for glaze. Shape into roll and bake at 350 °F for 1 hour. Drain well. Let cool for 20 minutes. Roll out pastry and wrap around the meat roll with the seam down. Glaze and bake for another 20 minutes or until crust is brown. Serves 6.

Notes:

Stir-Fry Steak - Quick & Easy

2/3 cup Soya sauce

1/3 cup sugar

1 clove garlic

2-3 Tbsp water

1/4 cup red wine

1/4 cup oil

2-3 lb steak, cut into bite size pieces

Combine the above ingredients and marinateall day.

Sauté the following vegetables:

3 oz fresh, sliced mushrooms

2-3 chopped celery stalks

1/2 green and/or red pepper – chopped

2 Tbsp butter

1 onion

Other vegetables – (e.g. snow peas, carrots, broccoli,

cauliflower)

1 Tbsp Soya sauce

Sauté the vegetables in butter. Remove from pan; add 1 Tbsp oil, and fry the steak for a few minutes until pink on inside. Add the vegetables and serve on brown rice or noodles. Serves 6-8.

Notes:

Beef Stroganoff - Quick & Easy

(Left over beef)

1 1/2 to 2 cups roast beef, cut into strips

3 Tbsp butter

1 clove garlic, put through garlic press

1 onion, minced

1/2 green pepper, cut into thin strips

1/4 pound mushrooms, sliced

1 Tbsp tomato paste

2 Tbsp flour

1/2 cup dry red wine (optional)

1/2 cup beef stock or 1 beef bouillon cube
dissolved in 1/2 cup boiling water

1/2 tsp paprika

Salt and pepper to taste

1 cup sour cream

Slice the cooked beef into narrow strips about 1 1/2 inches long. In a large deep skillet, melt butter and sauté garlic, onion, and green pepper until tender. Add mushrooms and the sliced cooked beef. Sauté 5 minutes more. Add tomato paste and sprinkle flour over the contents of the skillet, blending it in well. Add wine and beef stock, a little at a time, stirring constantly. Cook until mixture thickens. Add the seasonings, and lastly sour cream. Heat through gently until very hot, being careful, however, not to let the cream bubble. (If desired an additional 1 cup of beef stock may be use in this recipe and the wine omitted.) Serves 4-5.

Prime Rib Roast Beef

1 (5 lb) prime rib roast

Pepper

Garlic powder

1 tsp dry mustard

Rosemary

Thyme

Preheat oven to 400°F. Rub the ingredients on all sides. Place roast with fat side up. Turn oven down to 300°F - 325°F and bake uncovered until done as desired. Check by pressing the meat—if it's soft it is rare. The more well cooked the more solid it will feel to the touch.

Gravy: Put the drippings on high heat and add 1/4 cup flour; dissolve and brown in fat. Add 2 cups vegetable (potato or other) water and bring to a boil. Stir to prevent burning or lumps. Serves 6-8.

Yorkshire Pudding

This is a MUST as an accompaniment to Roast Beef in our family.

1 cup milk

2 eggs

1 Tbsp oil

1 cup flour

1 tsp salt

Preheat oven to 450°F. Blend just until smooth in blender. Put 1 tsp oil or drippings in each muffin tin. Place in oven that is heated until the fat is sizzling, and then add the pudding mixture. Bake at 450°F for 10 minutes, then turn oven down to 350°F for approximately 20 minutes until brown and puffy. Serves 6–8.

Sweet and Sour Meatballs

MEATBALLS:
1 1/2 lbs ground beef
1/4 cup bread crumbs
1/2 tsp salt
1/4 tsp ginger
1 tsp Soya sauce
1/4 tsp Tabasco sauce

Mix above ingredients and form into 1" meatballs and bake in 400°F oven for 20 minutes or until done.

SAUCE:
1/4 cup cider vinegar
3/4 cup water
1 can condensed beef broth
1 Tbsp ketchup
1 Tbsp Soya sauce
1 Tbsp molasses
1/4 cup brown sugar
8 oz pineapple chunks with juice
3 Tbsp cornstarch
2 medium zucchini (optional)
8 oz water chestnuts (optional)

Mix the sauce ingredients together, dissolving the cornstarch with water, and bring to boil. Add cooked meatballs and simmer 10 minutes.

1 can mandarin oranges
1/2 pt cherry tomatoes
Sesame seeds

Drain mandarin oranges and add them and the tomatoes just before serving. Sprinkle with sesame seeds. Serves 4-6.

Sloppy Joes

2 lbs ground beef

I small onion, minced

I tsp salt

1/8 tsp pepper

1/4 tsp chili powder

I tsp Worcestershire sauce

3/4 cup ketchup

I tsp dry mustard

1/4 cup brown sugar

8 sandwich rolls, split and heated

Brown beef, drain fat, add onion and spices. Add remaining ingredients. Simmer, stirring occasionally, 15-20 minutes. Serve on rolls. Serves 4.

Ribs On The Barbeque

Keep ribs in slabs. Cover with water (add onion, bay leaf, 12 peppercorns, I garlic clove to broth) and simmer, approximately 20 minutes until almost tender. Drain, let cool for 10 minutes (or longer), put on barbeque and cover with your favourite barbeque sauce. Serves 5-6.

N o t e s :

Barbecued Spareribs

4 lbs spareribs

1 sliced onion

2 cups ketchup

2 Tbsp Soya sauce

1 clove garlic

2 Tbsp Worcestershire sauce

1/4 cup vinegar

1/4 cup brown sugar

2 tsp dry mustard

1 tsp paprika

1/4 cup corn syrup or honey

FOR THE OVEN:

Cut spareribs into serving pieces. Brown them in a baking pan under the broiler, drain the fat. Blend all the other ingredients and pour over the ribs. Cover and bake in a moderate oven, (350 °F) for 1 3/4 hours. Spoon sauce over the ribs 2 or 3 times during baking. Uncover and bake an additional 15 minutes.

Notes :

Veal with Peppers and Mushrooms

Veal with an Italian touch. The scaloppini slices should be pounded to a thinness of 1/8", and should be young and of good quality for best results.

1 lb scaloppini of veal, cut into serving slices

Salt

Freshly ground black pepper

Flour

1 egg

6 Tbsp fine dried bread crumbs

6 Tbsp freshly grated Parmesan or Romano cheese

4 Tbsp olive oil

1/2 lb Italian sweet peppers cut into 1" chunks

1/4 lb mushrooms, sliced

1 clove garlic, put through garlic press

2 Tbsp dry sherry or marsala (optional)

1/8 tsp dried oregano

Salt and pepper to taste

Sprinkle the scaloppini with salt and pepper and dredge with flour. Beat the egg with 1 tablespoon of water. Mix together bread crumbs and grated cheese. Dip veal slices into beaten egg mixture and then into bread-crumb and grated-cheese mixture, coating each slice well. Heat the olive oil to very hot in a large skillet and brown the veal well on both sides. Remove veal, drain on paper towel and place in a 250°F oven to keep warm. Add peppers, mushrooms, and minced garlic to skillet and sauté in the remaining olive oil just until pepper and mushrooms are tender. Stir in sherry or marsala, add oregano, and salt and pepper to taste. Cook 5 minutes more. Arrange hot veal slices on a preheated platter and spoon mushrooms and peppers around veal. Serves 4-5.

Gourmet Curried Shrimp

A great easy dish for company.
If you want to make this Lo-Fat, cut down on butter and
use milk instead of cereal cream.

2 1/2 lbs shrimp, cooked

In frying pan, melt:

4 Tbsp butter

2 Tbsp curry

ADD AND SAUTÉ:

1 large onion, chopped

4 stalks celery, chopped

2 apples, diced

STIR TOGETHER AND ADD:

1/4 cup flour

2 tsp salt

1 tsp Accent

ADD:

3 cups cereal cream (or 3 cups milk)

1/2 cup shredded coconut

1 cup raisins

Bring to a boil and add shrimp. Serve with rice and Swedish Salad.
Serves 6.

Baked Cod - Quick & Easy

2 lbs cod fillets (or other solid flesh fish)

1/4 cup butter

1/2 cup flour

2 1/2 cup milk (1% or 2%)

2 tsp salt

Pepper (to taste)

1 large onion finely chopped

1 cup breadcrumbs or cracker crumbs

1 cup cheddar cheese grated

Preheat oven to 375°F.

Cut cod in cubes and place in a greased 13" x 9" baking dish.

Melt butter in saucepan; stir in flour until smooth and remove from heat, gradually stir in the milk. Return to heat and whisk mixture until thick. Add salt, pepper and onion. Pour over fish. Sprinkle with bread crumbs and cheese and bake at 375 °F for 30 minutes. Serves 6 to 8 people.

Notes :

Chili Con Carne

(low fat if you omit hamburger and add shredded cooked chicken)

3 Tbsp olive oil

2 cloves garlic, put through garlic press

2 large onions, diced fine

2 lbs ground beef

4 cups canned tomatoes with their liquid

1 (6 oz) can tomato paste

1 Tbsp chili powder

2 tsp salt

1 tsp oregano

1 bay leaf

2 (1 lb) cans red chili beans, un-drained (about 4 cups)

1 cup small-size ripe pitted olives

In a large, deep skillet, heat the oil and lightly sauté the garlic and the onions. Add the ground beef, crumbling it into small quantities as you do so, and fry it until it loses its red colour. Drain fat. Add the tomatoes, tomato paste, chili powder, salt, oregano and bay leaf. Simmer, uncovered for 1 hour. Add the red beans and the pitted ripe olives. Simmer, uncovered, for 30 minutes. Chili should be fairly thick. Correct seasoning, cool and refrigerate.

Next day, heat chili in a 350°F oven for 20-30 minutes or until chili is very hot.

Notes:

Meat Tips

Most meat is more tender if not overdone, except for pot roast. All roasts, (even if you like them well done) should be taken out of the oven while still slightly pink because they continue cooking after they are out of the oven.

After stewing a chicken for diced meat for casseroles, etc., let cool in broth before cutting into chunks; it will have twice the flavor.

To slice meat into thin strips, as for Chinese dishes, partially freeze and it will slice easily.

A roast with the bone in will cook faster than a boneless roast. The bone carries the heat to the inside of the roast.

Never cook a roast cold—let stand for at least an hour at room temperature. Brush with oil before and during roasting; the oil with seal in the juices.

For a juicier hamburger, add cold water to the beef before grilling, (1/2 cup to 1 pound of meat).

To freeze meatballs, place them on a cookie sheet until frozen. Place in plastic bags and they will stay separated so that you may remove as many as you want.

Don't despair if you've over-salted the gravy; stir in some instant mashed potatoes and you'll repair the damage. Just add a little more liquid to offset the thickening.

A leaf of lettuce dropped into the pot absorbs the grease from the top of the soup. Remove the lettuce and throw it away as soon as it has served its purpose.

For quick & easy and handy seasoning while cooking, keep on hand a large shaker containing six parts of salt and one of pepper.

Line crock-pot with foil for easy clean up.

DESSERTS

Apple Crisp

10 - 12 McIntosh apples

Grated zest of 1 orange

Grated zest of 1 lemon

2 tablespoons freshly squeezed orange juice

2 tablespoons freshly squeezed lemon juice

1/2 cup granulated sugar

2 teaspoons ground cinnamon

1 teaspoon ground nutmeg

TOPPING:

1 1/2 cups flour

3/4 cup granulated sugar

3/4 cup light brown sugar, packed

1/2 teaspoon kosher salt

1 cup oatmeal

1 cup cold unsalted butter, diced

Preheat the oven to 350 °F. Butter a 9" by 14" by 2" oval baking dish.

Peel, core, and cut the apples into large wedges. Combine the apples with the zests, juices, sugar, and spices. Pour into the dish.

To make the topping, combine the flour, sugars, salt, oatmeal, and cold butter in the bowl of an electric mixer fitted with the paddle attachment. Mix on low speed until the mixture is crumbly and the butter is the size of peas. Scatter evenly over the apples.

Place the crisp on a sheet pan and bake for 1 hour until the top is brown and the apples are bubbly. Serve warm.

Strawberry Cream Parfait

I cup cream cheese, softened

3/4 cup milk

I tsp vanilla

I envelope gelatin

2 Tbsp sugar

2/3 cup boiling water

I cup strawberries, halved

2 Tbsp orange liqueur or orange juice

1/4 cup sugar

In large bowl blend cream cheese until smooth. Gradually add milk and vanilla extract. Continue blending until smooth and creamy. In small bowl, combine gelatin and sugar. Add boiling water. Stir until dissolved. In food processor or blender, blend strawberries, liqueur or juice, and sugar. Blend gelatin mixture into cream cheese mixture. Add blended strawberries. Pour into parfait glasses. Chill until firm. Garnish with whipped cream and strawberries. Serves 6. (Use Splenda for lo-cal instead of sugar.)

N o t e s :

Fresh Blueberry Swirl

1 cup sugar

1/2 cup water

2 Tbsp lemon or orange juice

2 tsp grated lemon or orange rind

1 1/2 cups sifted flour

3 tsp baking powder

1 tsp salt

1/2 cup butter

1/2 cup rolled oats

1/2 - 2/3 cup milk

4 Tbsp butter, melted

2 cups fresh blueberries, sorted, washed and well drained

2 Tbsp sugar

Combine sugar, water, lemon or orange juice, and lemon or orange rind. Bring to a boil, cook 3 minutes, remove from heat, and set aside. Sift together the flour, baking powder, and salt. Cut in the butter with a pastry blender or two knives until the mixture resembles very coarse bread crumbs. Add rolled oats and then milk, 1/2 cup at first, then a tablespoon more at a time, stirring lightly until a stiff dough is formed. Gather the dough together, knead lightly, and roll out on a floured board or pastry cloth to form a rectangle of about 8" x 14".

Brush the dough with melted butter and cover with blueberries. Sprinkle with 2 tablespoons of sugar and roll up, like a jelly roll, starting at the 14" edge nearest you, and tucking in blueberries as you go. Seal edges by moistening dough with a little water, and cut roll into 12 slices a little over an inch wide, using a floured knife. Arrange slices, cut side down, in a buttered baking dish of approximately 7"x11"x 2". Pour cooled sugar and lemon syrup over and bake at 400°F for 25-30 minutes. Serve warm, either plain or with whipped cream or ice cream. Serves 6.

Crème Caramel

1 cup sugar

1/4 cup water

1/4 tsp cream of tartar

3 large eggs

1 egg yolk

1/2 cup sugar

1 tsp vanilla

1 cup whipping cream

1 cup milk

Combine first 3 ingredients in a heavy saucepan. Bring to a boil. Reduce heat and simmer, stirring frequently, until mixture turns a light golden brown (about 15 minutes). Pour syrup into four 10 oz custard cups; let cool.

Combine eggs, egg yolk, and 1/2 cup sugar with a wire whisk. Stir in vanilla. Combine whipping cream and milk in a saucepan. Heat until bubbles form around edge of pan. I gradually stir about one-fourth of hot milk mixture into egg mixture. Add to remaining hot milk mixture, stirring constantly. Pour evenly into custard cups. Place custard cups in a 13"x 9"x 2" pan. Add hot water to pan to a depth of 1". Cover with aluminum foil.

Bake at 325°F for 45 minutes or until a knife inserted in center of each cup comes out clean. Remove cups from water and let cool. Cover and chill at least 8 hours.

To serve, loosen edges of custard with a spatula, and invert onto individual plates, letting caramelized sugar mixture drizzle over top. Yield: 4 servings.

Cream Puffs

Cream Puffs and Mini-Éclairs make great finger food at a party. Stuff them with a variety of fillings. To keep pastries from becoming soggy serve them within one hour of filling.

1 cup boiling water

1/2 cup butter or margarine

1 cup flour

4 eggs

Boil water and butter in a saucepan. Put all the flour in and continue stirring until they come away from the side of the pot. Let cool for a few minutes and then put the eggs in one at a time, stirring until smooth after each egg. For small cream puffs or mini-éclairs put 1 tsp of mixture on an ungreased cookie sheet. For regular cream puffs make the mixture a size of a walnut. Bake at 425°F for 10 minutes and then turn oven down to 350°F and bake until puffy, dry, and golden brown.

EASY WHIPPED CREAM FILLING:

1 vanilla instant pudding mix –(prepare as per directions on box except using 1 cup milk instead of 2 cups)

FOLD IN:

1 cup of whipped cream

1/4 cup icing sugar

1 tsp vanilla

Slice top from puff and fill. Replace the top and sprinkle with icing sugar on top.

Cream Puffs...continued

PASTRY CREAM :
Makes about 1 1/2 cups

1 cup cereal cream

1 tsp vanilla

3 large egg yolks

1/4 cup sugar

2 1/2 Tbsp white flour

In a small saucepan over medium heat, scald the cream by bringing it just to a boil. Remove from heat, cover, add vanilla.

In a small bowl, whisk together the egg yolks, flour and sugar until smooth.

Slowly pour the hot cream/vanilla mixture into the egg mixture. Whisk until completely smooth and free of lumps.

Return the mixture to the saucepan, and place over medium heat. Bring the mixture to a boil, whisking constantly, and cook for another 2 minutes.

Remove the pastry cream to a bowl. Place a sheet of plastic wrap directly on top of the pastry cream to prevent a skin from forming.

Refrigerate until ready to use.

Notes :

Rice Pudding

1/2 cup regular rice

1 1/2 cups water

Cook for 15 minutes

Heat 3 3/4 cups whole milk. Add to rice. Mix together:

3/4 cup sugar

1 tsp salt

3 heaping Tbsp cornstarch

4 egg whites

4 Tbsp sugar

Add to above mixture. Cook until thickened. Add 4 slightly beaten egg yolks, 1/4 cup milk, and 1 tsp vanilla. Put into casserole. Top with meringue of 4 egg whites and 4 Tbsp sugar. Bake at 350°F until meringue is golden brown.

Tapioca Pudding

3 cups milk

3/4 cup sugar

1/2 cup tapioca

3 eggs

1 tsp vanilla

Soak tapioca in water at least one hour. Drain. Pour 2 cups of milk together with 1/2 cup sugar and tapioca. Boil till tapioca is transparent. Mix 3 eggs with 1/4 cup sugar and beat well. Mix in 1 cup milk. Mix with tapioca mixture and bake at 350°F for about 1 hour. Add vanilla just prior to serving.

CAKES

Orange Chiffon Cake

2 1/4 cups cake flour

1 1/2 cups sugar

3 tsp double-acting baking powder

1 tsp salt

1/2 cup cooking oil

5 unbeaten egg yolks

grated rind of 2 oranges

Juice of 2 oranges, plus water to make 3/4 cup

1 cup egg whites (7 or 8)

1/2 tsp cream of tartar

Sift together the first four ingredients into a mixing bowl. Make a "well" in the dry ingredients and add oil, egg yolks, orange juice, and rind in that order. Beat with a wooden spoon until perfectly smooth. In a large bowl, beat egg whites and cream of tartar until very stiff. Pour egg yolk mixture gradually over beaten egg whites and gently fold until blended. Pour into an ungreased 10" tube pan and bake approximately 65 minutes at 325°F. Invert pan to cool cake; loosen with a spatula. Fill layers of cake with the following:

FILLING:

Juice and rind of 1 orange

1 cup cold water

1 cup sugar

1 egg

3 Tbsp cornstarch

Mix sugar and cornstarch together. Add cold water to make a smooth paste. Add orange juice and rind and beaten egg. Beat until well blended. Cook until thick and clear. Spread between layers. Just before serving cover with whipped cream.

Swiss Chocolate Cake

1 cup water

1/2 cup margarine

1 1/2 squares unsweetened chocolate

2 cups flour

2 eggs

2 cups sugar

1/2 cup sour cream

1 tsp baking powder

1/2 tsp salt

Combine water, margarine, and chocolate in a saucepan, and bring to a boil. Remove from heat. Stir in combined flour and sugar. Add eggs, sour cream, soda, and salt. Mix well. Pour into greased 15 1/2"x 10 1/2" jelly roll pan. Bake at 375°F for 20-25 minutes. Frost while warm with milk chocolate frosting.

MILK CHOCOLATE FROSTING:

Melt 1/2 cup margarine, 6 Tbsp milk, and 1 1/2 squares unsweetened chocolate. Remove from heat. Add 4 1/2 cups icing sugar. Beat until smooth. Stir in 1 tsp vanilla.

Notes :

Devil's Food Cake

1/2 cup shortening

1 3/4 cups sugar

2 eggs

1/2 cup cocoa

2 1/4 cups cake flour

1 tsp baking powder

1/4 tsp salt

1 1/4 tsp baking soda

1/2 cup sour milk or buttermilk

1 cup boiling water

1 tsp vanilla

Cream shortening and add sugar gradually. Beat until fluffy. Add eggs and continue to beat. Add vanilla. Sift flour, measure and sift again with cocoa, salt, and baking powder. Add alternately with sour milk. Add baking soda to boiling water. When dissolved add all at once to mixture. Stir only enough to blend ingredients. This makes a very thin batter. Pour into greased pans. Bake at 350°F for 25-30 minutes. Makes two 8" layer cakes or one 9"x 13" cake.

Notes :

Banana Cake

1/2 cup butter

1 cup brown sugar

3 eggs

1 1/2 cups flour

1 tsp baking powder

1/4 tsp salt

1/3 cup milk

3 bananas

1 tsp baking soda

Cream butter; add brown sugar and well-beaten eggs. Sift together flour, baking powder, and salt. Begin to add alternately to first mixture with milk. Mash together bananas and add baking soda, making sure that the baking soda is dissolved. Add to first mixture. Pour into greased and floured 8"x 8"x2" pan and bake at 350°F for 35-45 minutes.

Notes:

Pavlova

6 egg whites

1 1/4 cups sugar

2 tsp vanilla

pinch of salt

1 Tbsp cornstarch

2 tsp vinegar

Beat egg whites until very stiff. Gradually add sugar and beat for 8 minutes. Add cornstarch, vanilla, vinegar and beat for 5 minutes. Heat oven to 350°F.

Place parchment paper on a cookie sheet, place the top part of a springform pan and set it on the paper. Pour the mixture into the pan.

Put in oven, turn oven back to 250°F and bake for 2 hours. When cool, remove from the springform, and transfer to a cake plate. Top with whipped cream, kiwi, fruit, or other fruits and toasted almonds. Serves 8.

Notes :

Schmoo Cake

6 egg whites

1/4 tsp cream of tartar

1 cup granulated sugar

6 egg yolks

1 Tbsp vanilla

1/2 cup flour

1 tsp baking powder

1 cup chopped pecans toasted

In a large bowl, beat egg whites with cream of tartar until soft peaks form. Add 1/2 cup sugar, 2 Tbsp at a time, beating until stiff peaks form. In another bowl, beat egg yolks and remaining sugar for 4 minutes or until pale and thick. Beat in the vanilla. Combine flour and baking powder, then stir this into the yolk mixture. Fold in 1/4 of the egg whites until combined; fold in remaining egg whites. Fold in pecans.

Scrape batter into 10 inch tube pan. Bake at 325°F for 50 minutes or until firm to the touch. Invert onto legs of pan. Let cool completely. Remove and cut cake horizontally in 3 layers

ICING:

2 1/2 cup whipping cream

2 Tbsp sugar

Whip cream and sugar. Spread 1 cup of whipped cream over the top of the bottom layer. Place second layer on bottom and repeat. Top with remaining layer, spreading the remaining cream over the top and sides. Refrigerate for at least 30 minutes or up to 24 hours.

BUTTERSCOTCH SAUCE:

1 1/2 cup brown sugar

1 cup whipping cream

2 Tbsp butter

In saucepan, wisk together brown sugar, cream and butter. Bring to a boil. Let cool completely. Drizzle some of the sauce over the cake. Serve the remaining sauce alongside.

Mocha Chiffon Cake

I cup cake flour

1/3 cup cocoa

3/4 cup sugar plus 2 Tbsp

1/3 cup water

3 egg yolks

1/4 tsp cream of tartar

I 1/2 tsp baking powder

1/2 tsp salt

5 Tbsp salad oil

I tsp vanilla

4 egg whites

Combine cake flour, cocoa, sugar, baking powder, and salt. Make a well in the center and pour in a mixture of salad oil, water, egg yolks, and vanilla. Beat until smooth.

Beat 4 egg whites and cream of tartar. Fold in chocolate mixture one quarter at a time. Bake in an angel food pan for 60 minutes at 325°F. Cool completely. Slice into six layers. Fill and frost with Mocha Cake Filling. Chill and then decorate with sweet shaved chocolate.

MOCHA CAKE FILLING:

1/3 cup sugar

2 Tbsp instant coffee

1/2 tsp vanilla

1/8 tsp salt

I pint whipping cream

topping

Combine the above and chill one hour. Beat until softly stiff. Fill and decorate the cake. Serves 8-10.

Orange Candy Cake

Good for Christmas or any time. Very nice fruit cake that keeps well.

1 lb orange candy, chopped (jelly type)

8 oz chopped dates

8 oz flaked coconut

2 cups pecans, chopped

1/4 cup flour

1 cup butter

2 cups sugar

4 eggs

1 tsp vanilla

1 tsp rum extract

2 1/4 cups flour

1 tsp salt

1 cup buttermilk

1/2 tsp baking soda

Mix first four ingredients and dust with flour. Cream butter; add sugar, eggs, vanilla, and rum. Sift flour and salt. Dissolve soda in buttermilk and alternate with flour mixture into the cream batter. Fold in first four ingredients and pour into a greased 10" tube pan. Bake at 325°F for 1 hour and 50 minutes.

MIX:

1/2 cup warm orange juice

2 cups icing sugar

Dissolve and pour on the cake while warm.

Coffee Cake

This can be doubled for a large cake.

1/4 cup butter

I cup brown sugar

2 eggs

I tsp vanilla

I tsp baking soda

I 1/2 tsp baking powder

I 1/2 cups flour

I cup sour cream

Cream butter and brown sugar together. Add eggs and vanilla. Sift together dry ingredients. Add alternately with sour cream.

TOPPING:

1/2 cup brown sugar

I Tbsp cinnamon

2/3 cup crushed nuts

Place half the batter in greased angel food cake pan. Sprinkle with half of the topping. Pour on rest of batter. Sprinkle with rest of topping. Bake at 350°F for 45 minutes. Serve warm with plenty of freshly brewed coffee.

Notes:

Cream Cheese Coffee Cake

1 (8 oz) package cream cheese, softened

2 Tbsp icing sugar

2 Tbsp lemon juice from concentrate

2 cups unsifted flour

1 tsp baking powder

1 tsp baking soda

1/4 tsp salt

1 cup granulated sugar

1/2 cup margarine or butter, softened

3 eggs

1 tsp vanilla extract

1 (8 oz) container sour cream

Cinnamon-Nut topping (below)

Preheat oven to 350°F. In small bowl, beat cheese, icing sugar, and lemon juice until smooth. Set aside. Stir together flour, baking powder, baking soda, and salt. Set aside. In large mixer bowl, beat granulated sugar and margarine until fluffy. Add eggs and vanilla. Mix well. Add dry ingredients alternately with sour cream. Mix well. Pour half of batter into greased and floured 10" tube pan. Spoon cheese mixture on top of batter to within 1/2 inch of pan edge. Spoon remaining batter over filling, spreading to pan edge. Sprinkle with Cinnamon-Nut topping. Bake 40-45 minutes or until wooden pick inserted near center comes out clean. Cool 10 minutes and remove from pan. Serve warm.

CINNAMON-NUT TOPPING:

Combine 1/4 cup finely chopped nuts,

2 Tbsp granulated sugar and 1/2 tsp ground cinnamon.

Carrot Cake with Chocolate and Pecans

CARROT CAKE:

3 1/4 cups sifted all-purpose flour

1 Tbsp ground cinnamon

1 tsp baking soda

1/2 tsp ground nutmeg

1/2 tsp salt

4 large eggs, at room temperature

2 cups granulated sugar

2 cups vegetable oil

2 tsp vanilla extract

3 1/2 cups grated carrots

1/2 cup coarsely chopped pecans

1/2 cup raisins

Cake: Preheat oven to 325°F. Lightly grease a 10" x 3" round cake pan and line the bottom with waxed paper and flour the sides. Stir together flour, cinnamon, baking soda, nutmeg and salt thoroughly. (Using paddle attachment on the blender:) Beat eggs at low speed until foamy. Gradually add sugar and beat until blended. Slowly add oil. Blend at medium for 1-2 minutes, until well emulsified. Beat in the vanilla. On low speed, beat in the carrots, pecans and raisins, mixing well after each addition. Mix in the flour just until combined. Bake cake for 60-65 minutes or until done with a cake tester. Remove from pan and cool right side up. Meanwhile prepare cream cheese frosting (next page.)

Assemble the cake: Remove paper circle from the bottom of the cake. Using a long serrated knife, trim the top of the cake, making sure that it is level. Horizontally slice the cake into two layers of equal thickness. Place one of the layers on a 10" cardboard cake circle. Spread 1 1/2 cups of the cream cheese frosting evenly over the top of the cake. Place the second layer of cake over the filling. Reserve 1 cup of the frosting for piping on the top of the cake. (Refrigerate the reserved frosting until it is time to decorate the cake) Frost the rest of the cake.

Carrot Cake with Chocolate and Pecans

CREAM CHEESE FROSTING:
4 1/2 cups sifted icing sugar
1/2 tsp ground cinnamon
1/2 tsp ground nutmeg
1 lb cream cheese, slightly softened
1 cup unsalted butter, softened
2 tsp vanilla extract

Cream Cheese Frosting: Stir together icing sugar, cinnamon and nutmeg. Sift the mixture onto a piece of waxed paper. Using the paddle attachment on the blender, combine cream cheese and butter. Beat at low speed for 30-60 seconds or until creamy. Gradually add the icing sugar mixture and beat until smooth. Beat in the vanilla. If the filling and frosting are very soft, cover the surface with plastic wrap and refrigerate until it has stiffened to spreading consistency.

GANACHE:
1 1/2 oz semi-sweet chocolate
2 Tbsp heavy whipping cream

Make the Ganache: Over medium heat, bring cream to a gentle boil. Pour the hot cream over the chocolate in a small bowl and let stand for 30 seconds; whisk until smooth. Cover the surface with plastic wrap and cool until room temperature.

DECORATION:
1 1/2 oz semi-sweet chocolate, coarsely grated
1 cup pecan pieces

To decorate: Spread chocolate shavings on the side of the cake until the side is completely covered. Place cake on a serving platter. Arrange pecans in an even layer over the top of the cake. Using a pastry bag fitted with a writing tip, pipe parallel lines of Ganache about 1" apart across the top of the cake. Turn the cake 90° and pipe more lines of Ganache, forming a lattice pattern. Changing to a pastry bag fitted with a star tip, pipe the reserved frosting around the top outside edge of the cake. Refrigerate the cake 1 hour before serving.

Pound Cake

1 cup butter or margarine, softened

1 (8 oz) package cream cheese, softened

3 cups sugar

6 large eggs

3 cups all-purpose flour

1/4 tsp baking soda

1 1/2 tsp vanilla extract

3/4 tsp lemon extract

Beat butter and cream cheese at medium speed with an electric mixer, about 2 minutes or until soft and creamy. Gradually add sugar, beating at medium speed 5-7 minutes. Add eggs, one at a time, beating just until yellow disappears.

Combine flour and soda. Gradually add to creamed mixture. Mix at lowest speed just until blended. Add extracts. Put into greased angel food pan and bake at 325°F for 60-75 minutes.

Notes:

Macaroon Cake

My Mom's recipe.

1/2 cup butter

1/2 cup sugar

3 egg yolks

1/2 cup milk

2 tsp baking powder

1 cup flour

Cream butter and sugar well. Add egg yolks. Sift flour and baking powder and stir in alternately with flour into batter. Pour into 9" x 9" greased pan.

FROSTING:

3 egg whites, beaten stiff

1/2 cup sugar

1 cup coconut

Add sugar to egg whites and fold in coconut and spread on cake batter. Bake at 350°F for 30 minutes or until meringue is golden.

Notes:

Poppy Seed Cake

1 cup butter

6 eggs

3 cups sugar

1 cup sour cream

1/2 tsp baking soda

1/2 tsp lemon extract

3 cups flour

1/4 cup poppy seeds – soaked for 1/2 hour in 1/4 cup rum

1 lemon, juiced with grated peel

Cream butter and sugar well. Add the eggs, extract, and lemon juice and peel. Sift dry ingredients together. Add the dry ingredients to the liquid gradually, mixing only until blended. Add the poppy seed rum mixture. Pour into greased angel food pan and bake at 325 °F for 60–70 minutes.

ICING:

2 cups icing sugar

1 Tbsp rum

1 Tbsp lemon juice

Add enough hot water to make a thin consistency and pour over cake.

Notes :

Baba Au Rum

CAKE:

Buy or bake an 8" tube form orange chiffon cake. On the day before the party, warm the orange chiffon cake in a 300°F oven for 8-10 minutes. (If you are baking your own orange chiffon cake, allow cake to cool for about 10 minutes after being taken from the oven, then proceed as directed.) Place warm cake on a serving plate, prick top and sides of cake all over with a toothpick, pushing toothpick well into the cake at all points, and spoon Rum Sauce onto cake as directed in recipe that follows.

RUM SAUCE (FOR BABA AU RUM)

1/2 cup sugar

3/4 cup apricot nectar

1/2 cup rum or 1 tsp rum extract

1 tsp lemon juice

Combine all ingredients in a saucepan and heat to boiling. Cook 3 minutes. Cool slightly and spoon over top and sides of warm Chiffon Cake. Allow first application of sauce to be absorbed, then repeat, pouring the Rum Sauce onto the cake only a little at a time until all the sauce has been used. Any Rum Sauce that accumulates in the bottom of the serving plate should be spooned up over the cake. Allow Baba to cool thoroughly and chill overnight. Next day, glaze the entire cake with the following Apricot Glaze:

APRICOT GLAZE (FOR BABA AU RUM):

3 Tbsp sugar

1 Tbsp cornstarch

1/2 cup apricot nectar

1 Tbsp rum

1 tsp lemon juice

Mix sugar and cornstarch together in saucepan. Add remaining ingredients and blend thoroughly. Cook over moderate flame, stirring frequently, until mixture thickens and becomes glossy and transparent. Cool. Glaze Baba all over and garnish, if desired, with candied cherries cut to form clusters of flowery petals. Baba Au Rum may be served with whipped cream that has been very lightly sweetened.

Strawberry Short Cake

2 cups flour

1 Tbsp baking powder

1/2 tsp salt

1/4 cup sugar

1/2 cup frozen unsalted butter (1 stick)

1 egg, beaten

1/2 cup plus 1 Tbsp light cream

1 pint of strawberries, hulled, sprinkle with 4 Tbsp sugar

Mix dry ingredients. Grate frozen butter into dry ingredients. Add liquid and knead gently (about 20 times). Pat out to about 3/4 inch; Form biscuits. Bake about 15-20 min at 400°F.

TOPPING:

1 cup whipping cream – beat till peaks

add 1/4 cup sugar

1 tsp of vanilla

Crush 2/3 of the strawberries, leave the rest whole

Top each of the biscuits with crushed strawberries and whipped cream if desired.

Notes:

Tweedies

A favourite of the Thiessens. It was actually used as a wedding cake for one of the clan.

BASE:

1/2 cup butter

2/3 cup sugar

1 1/3 cups flour

2 tsp baking powder

1/2 tsp salt

1/2 cup milk

2 squares semi-sweet chocolate

2 egg whites (well beaten)

Cream butter and sugar. Add dry ingredients alternately with milk. Fold in grated chocolate. Fold in egg whites. Bake at 350°F for 25 minutes in a 13" x 9" pan. If doubling the recipe, use jelly roll pan.

MIDDLE PART:

1/3 cup butter

2 egg yolks

2 cups icing sugar

2 squared semi-sweet chocolate, melted

Cream butter and egg yolks. Add icing sugar. Beat well. Spread over cooled base.

TOP:

Melt 8 oz chocolate chips, drizzle over top.

Torte Base for Sponge Cake

This is a double recipe. Cut in half for one Torte.

8 egg yolks

1/2 cup warm water

1 1/3 cups sugar

2 tsp vanilla

Mix for 10 minutes on high speed with electric mixer.

SIFT TOGETHER:

2 cups flour

4 tsp baking powder

and add gently to first mixture. Fold in:

8 egg whites, beaten until stiff

Pour into two 9" ungreased spring-form pans. Bake at 350°F for 1/2 hour. Cool. Cut into layers and fill with butter-cream or any other icing to make a variety of Tortes.

N o t e s :

Black Forest Cheesecake

1 1/2 cups chocolate cookie crumbs

1/2 cup margarine

Mix together and put as base in bottom of 10" spring-form pan.

4 (8 oz) pkgs cream cheese

1 1/2 cups sugar

1 Tbsp flour

4 eggs

1/3 cup kirsch or 1 tsp kirsch extract

Mix together and beat well. Pour over base. Bake at 350°F for 45-50 minutes. While still warm, mix:

1 cup sour cream

4 oz semi-sweet chocolate, melted

2 Tbsp kirsch

Spread on cheesecake. Refrigerate four hours. Garnish with whipping cream. Serves 10-12.

N o t e s :

Italian Cream Cheese Cake

1/2 cup butter

1 cup Crisco shortening

2 cups sugar

5 eggs

1 tsp baking soda

1 cup buttermilk

1 tsp vanilla

1 cup coconut

1 cup chopped nuts

2 cups plain flour

Have all ingredients at room temperature. Cream butter, Crisco and sugar. Add eggs, one at a time.

Sift flour and baking soda. Add flour mixture and buttermilk alternately with first mixture. Add flavoring, coconut, and nuts. Place in three 8" round greased and floured pans. Bake at 350°F for 35 minutes.

ICING:

1 (8 oz) pkg cream cheese

1/2 cup butter

1 tsp vanilla

diced maraschino cherries, drained

1 lb icing sugar

Cream first four ingredients together adding in the sugar last.

Cake Decorating Icing

1/3 cup shortening

1/3 cup margarine

1/4 tsp vanilla or almond flavor

3 cups icing sugar

1 1/4 Tbsp milk

Cream shortening and margarine. Gradually add icing sugar, beating well after each addition. Icing will be dry. Add milk and flavoring and beat until fluffy. This is a good icing for birthday cakes.

Whipped Cream

1 tsp unflavored gelatin

4 tsp cold water

1 cup heavy whipping cream

1/4 cup confectioners sugar

1/2 tsp vanilla extract

Combine gelatin and cold water in small saucepan. Let stand until thick. Place over low heat, stirring constantly just until gelatin dissolves. Remove from heat and cool slightly. Whip cream, sugar and vanilla until slightly thickened. While beating slowly, gradually add gelatin to whipped cream mixture. Whip at high speed until stiff. Yield: 2 cups. Refrigerate cake after decorating.

Notes:

COOKIES

Smartie Cookies

These make good cookies at Easter.

1 cup shortening

1 cup packed brown sugar

2 well-beaten eggs

1 tsp baking soda

1 1/2 cup Smarties

1/2 cup sugar

2 tsp vanilla

2 1/4 cups flour

1 tsp salt

Cream together shortening, sugar, and vanilla. Add well beaten eggs. Sift together flour, baking soda and salt. Add to above mixture. Combine 3/4 to 1 cup smarties into mixture. Roll into small balls, and garnish with the remainder of the smarties. Bake at 375°F for 10-15 minutes.

Sugar Cookies

1/2 cup butter or margarine

1 cup white sugar

2 eggs, beaten

2 1/4 cups flour

1 Tbsp baking powder

pinch of salt

3/4 tsp vanilla

Cream the butter or margarine. Add sugar and continue creaming. Add beaten eggs and mix well. Sift together flour, baking powder, and salt. Add to first mixture. Add vanilla. Chill dough and roll a little at a time on lightly floured board. Cut out with cookie cutters. Bake at 350°F for 10-15 minutes.

Gourmet Chocolate Chip Cookies

CREAM TOGETHER:

2 cups butter

2 cups white sugar

2 cups brown sugar

ADD:

4 eggs

2 tsp vanilla

ADD REMAINING INGREDIENTS:

4 cups flour

2 1/2 cups oatmeal (ground into flour in the blender)

1 tsp salt

2 tsp baking soda

24 oz chocolate chips

4 oz semi-sweet chocolate, grated

3 cups chopped nuts (optional)

Drop onto pan from small ice-cream scoop. Bake at 375°F for 10-12 minutes. Makes 5 dozen.

Notes:

Snickerdoodles

1/2 cup butter (or margarine)

1 cup sugar

1 tsp baking soda

1/4 tsp cream of tartar

1 egg

1/2 tsp vanilla

1 1/2 cups flour

2 Tbsp sugar

1 tsp ground cinnamon

In a medium mixing bowl, cream butter and 1 cup sugar until light. Add baking soda and cream of tartar. Beat till combined, scraping sides of bowl. Beat in the egg and vanilla till combined. Beat in as much of the flour as you can with the mixer. Stir in remaining flour. Cover and chill 1 hour.

Combine the 2 Tbsp Sugar and the cinnamon. Shape dough into 1-inch balls. Roll balls in sugar-cinnamon mixture to coat. Place 2 inches apart on an ungreased cookie sheet. Bake in a 375 degree F oven for 10-11 minutes or till edges are golden. Transfer cookies to a wire rack and let cool. Makes about 2 doz. cookies.

Notes :

PIES

TIP: *It's important to remember to refrigerate the dough for at least one hour before rolling out. Always roll in one direction FROM THE CENTER (not back and forth). Use as little flour as possible while rolling out.*

Pie Crust

6 cups flour

2 tsp salt

I lb lard

1/2 cup butter

2 eggs

I Tbsp vinegar

water (put eggs and vinegar in an 8 oz cup and fill to the top with water to make I cup liquid)

Cut lard and butter into dry ingredients. Beat eggs, vinegar, and water. Combine with first mixture and mix well. Refrigerate at least I hour. Can be kept in the refrigerator for I week, or divide into individual balls and freeze for future use. Yields 3 double crust pies.

Chocolate Wafer Crust

(This recipe is much more economical than using crushed chocolate wafers)

1/2 cup butter

I cup sugar

I egg

I 1/4 cups flour

1/2 cup cocoa

3/4 tsp baking soda

1/4 tsp salt

Cream butter, add sugar and egg and then the rest of the ingredients. Divide into two balls. Roll out and put in greased pie plates. Makes 2 pie crusts. Bake at 375°F for 8-10 minutes. Can be frozen. Fill with your favourite pie filling. Mocha or mint flavors are good with this.

Boston Cream Pie

*I also use this recipe for a base for my fruit flans.
One recipe makes two large flans.*

4 eggs

1 1/2 cups sugar

1 cup milk

2 tsp baking powder

2 tsp vanilla

2 cups flour

1/2 tsp salt

1/4 cup butter

Beat eggs and vanilla; add sugar, beat till very light. Add sifted dry ingredients. Heat milk and butter to boiling point and fold into batter. Don't beat. Pour batter into greased and floured 9"x 13"pan, or two 9" round cake pans. Bake for 40 minutes at 350°F. When cool, cut in two layers with a sharp knife and spread filling between layers.

FILLING:

1 1/3 cup sugar

1/2 tsp salt

4 cup scalded milk

3/4 cup flour

4 tsp vanilla

4 eggs beaten

Mix dry ingredients; gradually add scalded milk. Cook, stirring constantly until thick. Add small amount of hot mixture to egg. Return to pot and cook three minutes. Add vanilla. Let cool. Spread between layers. Sliced bananas or strawberries between the filling are nice varieties. Do not add them if you want to freeze the pie. Serve with whipped cream.

Apple Pie

I double crust unbaked

FILLING:

4 cups cored, peeled, sliced apples

1/2 – 3/4 cup sugar

3 Tbsp flour

1/2 – 1/4 tsp cinnamon

Mix apples with rest of the ingredients. Place into bottom crust. Cover with top crust. Prick top crust with fork to allow breathing.

Bake at 425°F for 10 minutes, then 375°F for 30 minutes or until brown and bubbling inside.

Custard Pie

I unbaked pie crust (9 inch)

MIX IN BLENDER:

3 eggs

2 cups whole milk (warmed in microwave)

1/2 cup sugar

I tsp vanilla

Pour into pie crust. Sprinkle with nutmeg. Bake at 325°F until custard is set. Test by inserting knife in center of pie. If it comes out clean the pie is done.

Chocolate Cream Pie

1 baked pie shell

2 cups milk, scalded

2 oz unsweetened chocolate

4 Tbsp flour

2 Tbsp cornstarch

1 cup sugar

1/4 tsp salt

2 or 3 egg yolks

2 Tbsp butter

1 tsp vanilla

Meringue or whipped cream to top

Melt chocolate in scalded milk. Mix flour, cornstarch, sugar, and salt. Add scalded milk gradually. Cook until thick, stirring constantly. Beat egg yolks, and into them stir a small quantity of the hot mixture. Cook for 2 minutes. Remove from heat, add butter and cool. Add vanilla. Pour into a baked pie shell and spread with a meringue made from egg whites, or top with whipped cream.

Notes:

Creamy Banana Pie

1 envelope unflavored gelatin

1/4 cup cold water

3/4 cup sugar

1/4 cup cornstarch

1/2 tsp salt

2 3/4 cups milk

4 egg yolks, beaten

2 Tbsp butter or margarine

1 Tbsp vanilla extract

4 medium, firm bananas

1 cup heavy cream, whipped

1 pastry shell (10"), baked

Soften gelatin in cold water; set aside. In a saucepan, combine sugar, cornstarch, and salt. Blend in the milk and egg yolks. Cook over low heat, stirring constantly, until thickened and bubbly, about 10-15 minutes. Remove from the heat. Stir in butter and vanilla. Cover the surface of custard with plastic wrap and cool to room temperature. Slice 3 bananas and fold into custard with 1/2 whipped cream. Spoon into pie shell. For garnish, spread with rest of whipped cream with banana slices. Chill until set, about 4-5 hours. Serve immediately. Yield: 8 servings.

N o t e s :

Flapper Pie

BASE:

14 Graham wafers, rolled fine (or 1 1/2 cups wafer crumbs)

1/4 cup melted butter

1/4 cup granulated sugar

1 tsp ground cinnamon

Mix together and remove 1/2 cup of mixture for top of pie, using the balance to line the bottom of pie plate.

FILLING:

2 cups milk

2 egg yolks

4 Tbsp cornstarch

1/2 cup granulated sugar

1 tsp vanilla

2 egg whites

3 Tbsp icing sugar

Combine milk, egg yolks, cornstarch, sugar, and vanilla. Cook until thick and spread over pie crust while hot. Beat egg whites until stiff and add icing sugar. Spread over filling. Sprinkle remaining crumbs on top and bake at 300°F for 20 minutes.

Notes:

Impossible Pie

An easy recipe for beginners. The pie forms its own crust while baking.

4 eggs

1/4 cup melted butter

1 1/2 cups sugar

1 tsp baking powder

1/2 cup flour

2 cups milk

4 oz shredded coconut

Beat eggs. Add all other ingredients. Mix well. Pour into two ungreased, deep 8" pie pans. Bake at 350°F for 40 minutes. Cool completely before serving.

Notes:

Lemon Meringue Pie

1 baked pie shell or 1 graham crust

GRAHAM CRUST:
1/4 cup butter

1 1/2 cup graham wafer crumbs

3 Tbsp sugar

FILLING:
1 1/4 cups sugar

1/3 cup cornstarch

1 1/2 cups water

3 egg yolks, beaten

2 Tbsp butter

2 tsp lemon rind, grated

1/3 cup lemon juice (approx. 2 lemons)

In the top section of a double boiler or a heavy aluminum pot, mix cornstarch, flour, and sugar. Add boiling water, stir, and cook over direct heat until there is no taste of raw starch. Beat egg yolks. Add to hot mixture, first adding a little cornstarch mixture to the eggs. Blend thoroughly. Cook 2 minutes until egg thickens. Remove from heat. Add butter, lemon juice, and rind. Cool slightly and pour into a baked pie shell. Cover with meringue.

MERINGUE:
2 or 3 egg whites

2 Tbsp fine sugar per egg white

2 Tbsp cold water

1/4 tsp cream of tartar

1/4 tsp vanilla

Beat egg whites, water, vanilla, and cream of tartar until stiff. Add sugar gradually and continue to beat mixture until very stiff. Spread over pie filling, touching the edges of the pie crust and bake at 300°F until golden brown.

Peanut Butter Cream Pie

1 baked 9" pie shell

PEANUT BUTTER CRUMBS:

2 cups icing sugar

1 cup crunchy peanut butter

Use hands to mix icing sugar and peanut butter together until fine crumbs are formed. Sprinkle 1/3 of crumb mixture in bottom of baked pie shell. Reserve 2/3 of crumbs.

FILLING:

2 egg yolks, beaten

1/2 cup sugar

2 Tbsp flour

3 Tbsp cornstarch

2 cups milk

1 Tbsp butter

1 tsp vanilla

1 cup whipping cream

Combine sugar, flour, and cornstarch. Add to beaten egg yolks. Mix to form a smooth paste. Add milk and cook, stirring constantly until thickened. Remove from heat and stir in butter and vanilla.

Pour cooked filling into baked pie shell. When cool, sprinkle with 1/3 of the crumbs. Top with whipped cream, add remaining 1/3 of crumbs.

Pecan Pie

1 unbaked pie shell

FILLING:

1 1/4 cups corn syrup

1 cup brown sugar

1/4 cup melted butter

Boil the syrup, brown sugar and butter in microwave. Then add the following ingredients:

4 eggs, slightly beaten

1 tsp vanilla

1 1/2 cups chopped pecans

Put 1 cup of the pecans on the bottom of an unbaked pie shell and then pour the liquid on top with the rest of the pecans. Bake in the oven until the filling is almost solid and a knife comes out clean. Bake at 350°F for 45-50 minutes.

Notes:

Pumpkin Pie

1 unbaked pie shell

1 cup canned pure pumpkin

1/4 cup white sugar

1/2 cup brown sugar

1/2 tsp salt

1/2 tsp nutmeg

1/2 tsp ginger

1 tsp cinnamon

1 Tbsp molasses or corn syrup

2 eggs beaten

1 1/4 cup evaporated milk

Mix together all ingredients. Heat in microwave only until warm. Pour into unbaked pie shell. Bake at 350°F for 30 minutes or until knife inserted comes out clean.

Serve with plenty of sweetened whipped cream.

Notes:

Pumpkin Pie with Meringue

1 (9 inch) unbaked pie crust

FILLING:

1 (16 oz) can mashed, cooked pumpkin

3 large egg yolks

1 (14oz) can sweetened condensed milk

1/2 cup flaked coconut

1/4 cup water

1 tsp ground cinnamon

1/2 tsp ground ginger

1/2 tsp ground nutmeg

Dash of salt

1/4 tsp cream of tartar

3 egg whites

1/2 cup sugar

Place pie crust in a 9" pie plate; trim off excess pastry along edges. Fold edges under a crimp. Prick bottom and sides of pie crust with a fork. Bake at 425°F for 5 minutes on lowest oven rack.

Combine pumpkin, egg yolks, sweetened condensed milk, and next six ingredients; pour into pie crust. Shield crust with aluminum foil, and bake at 400°F for 30 minutes in center of oven.

Beat egg whites and cream of tartar at high speed with an electric mixer until foamy. Gradually add sugar, 1 Tbsp at a time, beating until stiff peaks form and sugar dissolves (2-4 minutes). Spread over hot filling, sealing to edge of pastry. Shield crust, and bake at 325°F for 25-28 minutes or until golden brown; cool on a wire rack. Yield: one 9" pie.

Rhubarb Crumble Pie

1 unbaked 9 inch pie shell

4 cups rhubarb finely cut
1 1/2 cups white sugar
1/3 cup flour
1 cup sour cream

1/2 cup flour
1/2 cup brown sugar
1/4 cup soft butter

Arrange rhubarb in unbaked pie shell. Mix together sugar and flour. Stir in sour cream and pour evenly over rhubarb. Combine remaining ingredients until crumbly and sprinkle on top. Bake in a 450°F oven for 15 minutes. Then bake an additional 30 minutes at 350°F or until fruit is tender, filling is set, and crumbs are golden.

Rum Cream Pie

1 baked pie shell – or chocolate wafer crust

FILLING:
1 envelope gelatin
1/4 cup cold water
6 Tbsp sugar
3 egg yolks (beaten till fluffy)
1/4 cup rum
1 cup whipping cream
Semi-sweet chocolate - shaved

Dissolve gelatin in cold water and place this container into a larger bowl of hot water. Add sugar gradually into beaten eggs. Add gelatin. Stir in rum. Whip and fold into egg mixture. Pour into a baked pie shell or chocolate wafer crust. Shave chocolate on top of pie. Fills one 9" baked pie shell. Refrigerate for at least 3 to 4 hours before serving.

Crème de Menthe or Grasshopper Pie

Substitute the following instead of Rum to the preceding recipe:

2 oz crème de menthe

1 oz crème de cocoa

Same as above, this is good with chocolate crumb shell.

Strawberry Cream Pie

CRUST:

1 cup flour

2 Tbsp icing sugar

1/2 cup margarine

Mix until crumbly. Press into a buttered pie plate. Prick with a fork and bake at 400°F for 8-10 minutes. Cool.

FILLING:

4 oz cream cheese

1/2 cup icing sugar

1/2 tsp vanilla

1 cup whipping cream

1 pkg Oetker fruit glaze

Fresh strawberries

Beat cheese, vanilla, and sugar. Whip cream and add to cheese mixture. Pour into cooled shell. Place fresh strawberries on top. Heat glaze (available in specialty sections in supermarkets), and pour over berries. Refrigerate until serving.

Butter Tarts

CRUST:
2 1/4 cups pastry flour
1/2 tsp salt
3/4 cup lard or vegetable shortening
1 tsp lemon juice
1 egg
4 Tbsp to 6 Tbsp cold water

FILLING:
1 cup raisins
1/2 cup hot water
1/4 cup unsalted butter, room temperature
1/2 cup dark brown sugar, packed
2 eggs
1 tsp vanilla extract
1/2 tsp white vinegar
dash cinnamon
1/4 cup corn syrup
1/2 cup maple syrup
pinch of salt (optional)

Preheat oven to 400° F. For pastry, combine flour and salt and cut in lard until coarse and crumbly. Whisk lemon juice and egg and mix into dough until it just comes together. Wrap and keep at room temperature while preparing filling.

For filling, soak raisins in hot water for 10 minutes and drain. Set aside. Cream together butter and sugar and stir in eggs. Mix in vanilla, vinegar and cinnamon. Whisk in corn syrup and maple syrup.

On a lightly floured surface, roll out pastry about 1/4 inch thick. Cut 4 inch rounds from pastry and line ungreased muffin tins, pressing in to ensure pastry gets into corners. Sprinkle a few raisins in each shell and pour filling over, coming only halfway up. Bake tarts for 18 to 22 minutes, until filling is set. Allow to cool before removing from tin.

Butter tarts will keep up to a week in an airtight container (if they last that long). Makes about 14 small tarts.

BREADS & ROLLS

French Bread

2 pkg yeast or instant yeast as directed

1/2 cup warm water

2 cups hot water

3 Tbsp sugar

1 Tbsp salt

4 Tbsp vegetable oil

6 cups flour

1 egg white

Sesame seeds

Dissolve yeast in 1/2 cup warm water. Let stand for 10 minutes. In large bowl, combine 2 cups hot water, sugar, salt, oil, and half of the flour; beat well. Stir in dissolved yeast. Stir in remaining flour. Mix well with hands. Rest for 10 minutes. Knead again. Allow to rest again for 10 minutes. Knead again, and repeat 3 or more times. Turn out dough onto floured board. Knead once or twice until lightly coated with flour. Divide dough in half. Roll each into a 9"x 12" rectangle. Starting at long edge, roll loosely as for jelly roll. Seal edge. Place both rolls on one large baking sheet. Gash top of each loaf diagonally 3 times with a sharp knife. Brush with beaten egg white. Sprinkle with sesame seeds. Let rise 30 minutes. Pre-heat oven to 450°F and place a pan of boiling water on a lower shelf in the oven. Bake at 450°F for 10 minutes, then reduce temperature to 300°F and bake for about 15 minutes or until golden brown. Yields 2 loaves.

Notes :

Raisin Bread

4 cups warm milk
(or powdered milk mixed with warm water)

5 eggs

I cup sugar or honey

3 pkg yeast

I cup melted margarine or shortening

12-16 cups of flour

2-3 cups raisins

Cinnamon

2 tsp salt

Mix eggs, milk, and melted shortening in the blender. Prepare yeast as directed. Add to other liquids. Put 8 cups of flour, salt, and sugar into large mixing bowl. Add the raisins and then the liquids and knead very well. This is an important step. Then slowly add flour and keep kneading until you have medium dough that does not stick to your hands. It will start rising as you knead. Let rise for 20 minutes. Knead well again. Let rise until double the bulk. Divide dough into 6 or 7 parts. Roll out one at a time, sprinkle with cinnamon, and roll up as jelly roll. Pinch together well and place in a greased bread pan. Let rise again until double in bulk. Bake at 400°F for 20-30 minutes or until golden brown. Brush with melted butter. Yields: 7 loaves.

Notes:

Cinnamon Buns

This recipe is good basic sweet dough to use for cinnamon buns, doughnuts and other breakfast rolls.

Use a 2 lb bread machine for mixing, or you can knead it by hand.

6 1/4 cups flour

2 pkg yeast

14 oz milk (warmed slightly)

3 eggs

1/2 cup butter (melted)

1/2 cup sugar

1/2 tsp salt

DOUGH (BREAD MACHINE):

Place all the ingredients into the machine; mix a bit with a wooden spoon since it's more than the usual mixture. Place on dough setting.

DOUGH (HAND PREPARATION):

Combine 1/2 the flour, instant yeast, salt, and sugar into a large mixing bowl. Mix the liquids including melted butter and add to the flour mixture. Beat or knead very well. Add additional flour to make soft dough. Knead well. Let rise for 20 minutes. Knead well again and let rise until double in bulk.

N o t e s :

Cinnamon Buns...continued

FILLING:

Soft butter

Brown sugar

Cinnamon

Raisins (optional) soften in water and drain

Roll out dough into a rectangle to a thickness of about 1/4 inch. Butter the surface of the dough lightly. Spread brown sugar lightly over the buttered surface. Sprinkle cinnamon over the surface - to taste. Add raisins if desired. Roll up as in a jelly roll. Cut into 3/4 inch widths. Place on buttered or Pam sprayed pan. Allow to rise (covered) until doubled in size. Bake at 400°F for about 12 minutes. Yields: 16 to 20 cinnamon rolls.

ICING:

A mixture of icing sugar, a few spoons of water and 1 tsp vanilla. Make into medium consistency and drizzle over hot cinnamon buns.

SWEET BUNS:

Pinch together small pieces of dough, put on pans, cover with a dish towel and keep warm. (The oven at 100°F is great.) Let rise until double in size. Bake at 400°F for about 10 minutes.

Notes:

Philadelphia Sticky Buns

This is another easy all-purpose recipe for rolls, cinnamon buns, and hot cross buns. Just add mixed fruit and raisins.

DOUGH:

1 cup warm milk

3/4 cup sugar

1 1/2 tsp salt

3/4 cup butter

3/4 cup warm water

3 pkg yeast

3 eggs

7 1/2 cups flour

Mix warm water with yeast and let stand for 10 minutes. Put in blender milk, sugar, eggs, and salt. Add yeast mixture. Put flour in large mixing bowl. Add liquid and knead until smooth, approximately 10 minutes. Let rise until double in bulk.

FILLING:

Cream 3/4 cup butter and 3/4 cup brown sugar. Spread on three 9"x 9"baking pans. Sprinkle with cinnamon and pecans. Roll out dough to 1/4 inch thickness. Spread soft butter, 1 1/2 cups brown sugar, raisins, and roll up in the jelly roll fashion. Cut in 1" slices and arrange on top of the filling. Bake at 400°F for approximately 10 minutes. Yields: 2 dozen.

QUICK & EASY
BREADS

Date-Nut Bread

1 cup pitted dates, cut into 1/4 inch pieces

1 cup sugar

1 cup boiling water

1/2 cup vegetable shortening

2 eggs, well beaten

2 cups sifted all purpose flour

1 1/2 tsp baking soda

1/2 tsp salt

1 cup walnuts, coarsely chopped

1 tsp vanilla extract

Place dates and sugar in a large mixing bowl. Add vegetable shortening to boiling water and keep water simmering until shortening is melted. Pour this mixture immediately over dates and sugar, and stir until sugar is dissolved. Cool slightly. Add eggs, beating mixture well. Combine flour, baking soda, and salt. Sift into date mixture, stirring until blended. Batter may be slightly lumpy. Add walnuts and vanilla. Turn batter into a greased 9" x 5" loaf pan or into 2 well-greased cylindrical coffee tins, about 8" long and 3" in diameter, filling each tin 2/3 full. Lacking coffee cans of these dimensions, use ordinary tin cans, as tall as you can get them, measuring from 2 1/2 to 3 inches in diameter. Remove rough edges around rim, wash thoroughly, and grease well. Fill each tin 2/3 full, using as many as are necessary to use up batter. Bake tins, (standing them upright on lower shelf in oven) at 325°F until batter has risen to a hump, is well browned, and springs back to touch. Time will vary depending on size of baking utensil, the regulation 9" x 5" loaf taking about 1 hour.

Notes:

Cinnamon Loaf

1/4 cup margarine

1 cup white sugar

1 egg

2 cups flour

1 tsp baking powder

1/2 tsp baking soda

1/2 tsp salt

1 cup milk

2 Tbsp vinegar

2 tsp vanilla

2 Tbsp cinnamon

3 Tbsp brown sugar

Combine margarine, sugar, and egg in a bowl; add sifted dry ingredients. Then add milk, vinegar, and vanilla. Combine cinnamon and brown sugar in a separate bowl. Line greased loaf pan with wax paper. Alternate layers of batter and sugar mixture. Run a knife through to marble. Bake in 350°F oven for about 1 hour.

Notes:

Lemon Loaf

1/2 cup shortening

1 cup sugar

2 eggs

1/2 cup milk

Rind of lemon

1 1/2 cups flour

1 tsp baking powder

1/2 tsp salt

1/2 cup walnuts

Cream sugar and shortening. Add eggs and dry ingredients. Add milk. Bake at 350°F for one hour. Mix:

Juice of 1 lemon

1/4 cup sugar

Pour over loaf while still in pan and still warm.

Notes :

Bran Muffins

Batter can be kept refrigerator for a week.

2 cups boiling water

2 cups Nabisco 100% bran cereal

1 cup shortening

3 cups white sugar

4 eggs

4 cups buttermilk

4 cups Kellogg's All Bran

5 cups flour

5 tsp baking soda

1 1/2 tsp salt

Raisins or dates

Pour boiling water over Nabisco 100% bran and cool. Cream shortening and add sugar. Add eggs, buttermilk and beat well. Add the cooked mixture and then add Kellogg's All Bran, flour, baking soda, salt, and raisins or dates. Pour into muffin tins and bake at 400°F for 15-20 minutes. Yields: 5 dozen.

Notes:

Banana Muffins

2 lbs bananas

3/4 cup butter

1 cup brown sugar

1 cup white sugar

3 eggs

1/2 cup sour cream

2 tsp vanilla

3 1/2 cups flour

1/4 tsp salt

4 tsp baking powder

1 Tbsp baking soda

Mash 1 1/2 lbs bananas and cut remaining 1/2 lb in chunks (do not mash).

Cream butter, sugar, eggs, sour cream, and vanilla together. Mix with bananas.

Sift dry ingredients and mix together by hand with banana mixture until just mixed (don't stir too much).

Mix 24 hours before using and refrigerate.

Fill each segment of paper lined muffin pan to about 3/4 full. Bake for 15 – 20 minutes at 375°F.

Notes:

Oatmeal and Blueberry Muffins

1 cup rolled oats

1 cup sour milk

1 cup flour

1 tsp baking powder

1/2 tsp baking soda

1/2 tsp salt

1/2 cup brown sugar, lightly packed

1 egg, beaten

1/4 cup melted butter

1 cup blueberries or raisins

Preheat oven to 375°F. Combine rolled oats and milk, and set aside. Combine flour, baking powder, baking soda, and salt. Add brown sugar. Stir beaten egg and melted butter into rolled oat mixture. Add to dry ingredients, stirring with fork. Add blueberries carefully. Fill two muffin pans with cupcake liners. Divide the batter among them. Bake at 375°F for 15-20 minutes. Yield: 12 large muffins.

Notes:

TRY

Oatmeal Banana Muffins

1 1/2 cup flour

1 cup rolled oats

2 tsp baking powder

1 tsp baking soda

1/2 tsp salt

1 egg

1/4 cup oil

1/2 cup sugar or Splenda

1/2 cup milk

1 cup mashed banana

Preheat oven to 375°F. Combine the oil, milk, egg and mashed bananas. Combine the dry ingredients. Carefully stir the liquids into the dry ingredients. Fill the muffin pans with cake liners. Divide the batter among them. Yield: 12 large muffins.

Biscuits Supreme

2 cups sifted all-purpose flour

4 tsp baking powder

1/4 tsp cream of tartar

1/2 tsp salt

2 tsp sugar

1/2 cup soft butter

2/3 cup milk

Sift together dry ingredients; cut in butter until mixture resembles coarse oatmeal. Add milk all at once and stir with fork only until blended. Knead ten times on lightly floured board. Roll or pat out dough to 1/2 inch thickness. Cut with floured biscuit cutter and place on lightly buttered baking sheet. Bake in hot oven at 450°F for 10-12 minutes. Yield: 12 biscuits.

Biscuits – Make Ahead

These wonderful biscuits can be baked immediately or frozen and baked as needed.

1 Tbsp instant yeast

5 cups flour

5 Tbsp sugar

1 Tbsp baking powder

1 tsp baking soda

1 tsp salt

1 cup butter or margarine

2 1/4 cups buttermilk

In a large bowl mix flour, yeast, sugar, baking powder, baking soda and salt. Cut in butter to form a crumbly mixture. Stir in buttermilk and mix just enough to hold dough together. Roll dough 3/4 inch thick on floured surface. Cut out biscuits with the top of a glass or a cutter and prick tops with fork.

If you are using immediately, let biscuits rise until double in bulk.

Otherwise freeze separately on cookie sheet. After biscuits are frozen, stack and wrap well.

Before baking, thaw and let rise until doubled in size - about 1 hour Bake at 425°F for 15 minutes on a lightly greased cookie sheet. Makes 3-4 dozen.

Alternative: Grated cheddar cheese may be added to soft dough for flaky cheese biscuits.

Tea Scones

5 cups flour

1 cup sugar

3 Tbsp baking powder

1 tsp baking soda

1 1/2 cups shortening or butter

4 eggs

1 cup buttermilk

2 cups raisins or currants or dried cherries,

or dried cranberries

Rind of 1 orange

1 tsp salt

Sift dry ingredients together. Cut in shortening into fine crumbs. Beat eggs and blend with milk. Combine wet and dry ingredients. Knead dough slightly to form a soft dough for rolling. Roll mixture to 3/4" thickness and cut into 3" rounds. Bake at 375°F for 20-30 minutes. Serve with homemade preserves and butter.

Corn Bread or Johnny Cake

1 cup cornmeal

1 cup flour

1/2 cup sugar

1/2 tsp baking soda

1/2 tsp salt

3 tsp baking powder

1/2 cup sour cream

1/2 cup milk

1 egg

Mix dry ingredients. Mix egg, sour cream and milk. Make a well in flour mixture and add the milk mixture just until moistened. Put into greased 8" x 8" pan. Bake at 350°F for 20 minutes.

HOLIDAY FOODS

Usually there are extra people around during the holiday seasons. Take advantage of fellowship by cooking together. I'm not a person who discourages help when preparing food... its fun having more than one in the kitchen!

"O' Henry Bars" aare one of the family favourites when it comes to Christmas baking. These can be made "assembly line" style... the person dipping in the chocolate is usually the lucky one to lick their fingers when it's all over.

A Christmas tradition for French Canadians is "Tourtiere" on Christmas Eve. We've adopted this tradition and add a cheese fondue. We also have a regular meat fondue every New Year's Eve. We find that this makes mealtime last a long time; sometimes we're at the table several hours! (Meanwhile, we've had grandchildren, and have had to adapt that tradition slightly!)

Of course, we can't forget the traditional turkey dinner with all the trimmings. I try to make vegetable and salad dishes that can be made ahead of time so that I can enjoy the family.

Holiday times are eating times... so make the BEST of them!

Shortbread

1 cup butter

1/2 cup icing sugar

2 cups flour

3 Tbsp rice flour

Cream butter and add icing sugar. Add both flours. Roll out and cut into shapes. Decorate with candied cherries if desired. Bake at 300°F for approximately 8-10 minutes until slightly changed in colour. Do not over-bake.

O' Henry Bars

1 cup corn syrup

1/2 cup sugar

2 cups peanut butter

1 tsp vanilla

1 cup peanuts

2 cups Rice Krispies

2 cups Cornflakes

1 (12 oz) pkg chocolate chips

3 oz unsweetened chocolate

1/3 block paraffin wax

Heat sugar and corn syrup until sugar melts. Add 1 cup peanut butter and vanilla to mixture. Pour over and mix well with Cornflakes, Rice Krispies and the remainder of the peanut butter, (more can be used if desired). Press into a lightly greased 9" x 13" pan. Do not make it too thick. Cut into squares and let cool. Carefully melt together paraffin, chocolate chips, and chocolate. Mix well and dip the squares on both sides and place on waxed paper to cool.

FONDUES

Chocolate Fondue

This is fun at Christmas time.

1/2 lb (250g) bittersweet or semisweet chocolate

1/2 cup half and half cream

1/4 cup corn syrup

I tsp vanilla

2 Tbsp coffee or orange flavored liqueur

Assorted fruits and cake

Coarsely chop chocolate. Combine chocolate, cream, and corn syrup in a 4-cup measuring cup. Microwave, uncovered on high for 2 1/2 minutes or until chocolate is almost melted. Stir twice during cooking. Then stir in vanilla and liqueur until mixture is smooth. Serve warm with pieces of fruit and cake. To reheat, microwave uncovered on medium for about 3 minutes, stirring occasionally, being careful not to scorch the chocolate. Make 1 1/3 cups, about 6 servings.

Notes:

Meat Fondue

Cut sirloin beef, boneless chicken, or pork tenderloin into 1" bite size cubes.

Make a variety of sauces, e.g. sweet and sour, mustard, and horseradish. There are also many good bottled varieties on the market.

The following is my favourite mushroom sauce, which is great with beef fondue, or any beef roast.

SAUCE DUXELLES:

2 Tbsp butter or margarine

3 cups finely diced mushrooms

2 Tbsp minced onion

1/2 cup dry Madeira or sherry wine (optional)

1 can beef broth or consommé

1 dash of pepper

2 Tbsp flour

1 Tbsp melted butter or margarine

Melt 2 Tbsp butter or margarine in skillet over medium heat. Add mushrooms and onion. Cook, stirring frequently, for 5 minutes. Add wine. Cook for 1 minute. Add beef broth and pepper. Simmer 5 minutes or until liquid is reduced to half. Make thick by mixing flour with 1 Tbsp melted butter. Add to sauce, stirring until sauce thickens. Correct seasoning to taste. Make about 3 cups.

Swiss Fondue

Use as an appetizer if you wish.

1 garlic clove, crushed

2 Tbsp butter

1 Tbsp Dijon mustard

2 Tbsp all purpose flour

2/3 cup dry white wine (nonalcoholic wine can be used)

1 lb (500g) grated Swiss cheese

Measure garlic, butter, mustard, flour and wine into a 3 L microwave safe casserole dish. Microwave, uncovered, on high for 2 minutes. Whisk twice during cooking. Continue cooking on high until mixture bubbles slightly, about 30 seconds. Whisk, and then stir in cheese. Microwave, uncovered, on medium for 8 minutes. Stir every 2 minutes. Serve hot with cubes of crusty bread, pieces of apple, and raw vegetables. To reheat, microwave uncovered on medium for about 5 minutes, stirring occasionally. Makes 2 1/3 cups, about 6 servings.

Notes :

My Favourite Tourtiere

This is a little more work — but worth the effort.

I double pastry shell

2 medium apples

1/4 cup lemon juice

2 Tbsp water

2 Tbsp cooking oil

1/2 lb pork sausages

I large onion, chopped finely

I clove garlic, minced

I lb ground lean pork

1/2 lb ground veal or beef

I 1/2 tsp salt

1/4 tsp pepper

1/2 tsp celery salt

1/2 tsp allspice

I egg yolk

I Tbsp water

Peel and slice apples into saucepan. Add lemon juice and 2 Tbsp water. Cover and cook until apples are very tender. Mash if necessary to make a smooth sauce. Heat oven to 450°F. Have ready a 9" pie pan. Heat oil in heavy skillet. Add sausage pieces and cook until browned and cooked through. Lift out with a slotted spoon and set aside. Add onion and garlic to fat left in skillet and cook gently 3 minutes, stirring. Add pork and veal and cook until lightly browned. Drain the fat. Remove from heat and stir in applesauce and seasonings.

Line pie pan with half of pastry. Fill with meat mixture and sprinkle with sausage pieces. Top with remaining pastry, sealing edges well and fluting. Cut a large slit in the top crust to let the steam escape. Beat egg yolk and I Tbsp water together and brush over top crust (not the edge). Bake at 450°F for 20 minutes. Reduce oven temperature to 350°F and bake about 60 minutes or until crust is very brown. Serve hot or cold. Serves 6.

MENNONITE RECIPES

It's fun to share ethnic foods with each other. Every family has its own ethnic traditions, often foods others never had the opportunity to experience. Willard and I both come from Mennonite backgrounds and our whole family enjoys many traditional Mennonite foods.

At Easter time, our family eats ham with fried potatoes or a potato salad along with our favourite soup – Pluma Moos. This meal is accompanied by homemade Easter bread, my personal favourite. My mother's home-made mustard recipe served with the ham completes the meal.

A hot summer day favourite for us is watermelon and roll kuchen. Our family pours lots of corn syrup on the roll kuchen for extra fla-vor…and calories.

Grandma's Perogies were a MUST when she came to visit. We serve them with a cream sauce, made with whipping cream, and lots of apple-sauce and/or rhubarb sauce. These sauces bring tartness and flavor to an otherwise bland dish.

Roll Kuchen

1 cup heavy cream

4 eggs

2 1/2 – 3 cups flour

2 tsp baking powder

1 tsp salt

Sift flour, salt, and baking powder into mixing bowl, make a well. Add other ingredients. Knead well. Add a bit more flour if the dough is too soft to handle. Let stand at room temperature for at least an hour. Roll out to 1/8"- /4" thick on floured board. Cut into 3"x5" strips. Heat oil in a large Dutch Oven filled with 1 1/2" to 2" vegetable oil. This tastes best served with watermelon.

Notes:

Bubbat

*This is a traditional Mennonite accompaniment to chicken and turkey.
It is very similar to a muffin batter.*

1/2 cup soft margarine or shortening

2 eggs

1 cup milk

Put into the blender and blend until smooth.

SIFT:

2 cups flour

1/2 cup sugar

1 tsp salt

3 tsp baking powder

ADD:

1 1/2 cups raisins *(TRY APPLES INSTEAD)*

Pour the liquid ingredients into the dry and mix with spoon until blended. Bake in a greased 9" x 13" pan at 350°F for 25 minutes or until done. Serve hot with roast chicken. Also, you can put the batter into muffin tins and serve as muffins. Serves 6.

Notes:

Peppermint Cookies

(An ingredient sometimes difficult to find is baking ammonia which can sometimes be found in Mennonite specialty food stores)

3 cups sugar

1 1/2 cup butter

2 cup sour cream

4 eggs

4 cups flour

3 tsp baking powder

Combine butter and sugar well, add eggs one at a time and then sour cream. Sift together flour and baking powder and add to the mixture. Put in fridge overnight.

IN THE MORNING ADD:

6 tsp baking ammonia

4 tsp peppermint extract

Make a soft dough by adding 2 3/4 cups flour. Now let it rest at room temperature for 1 to 2 hours.

Roll out 1/4 inch thick. Use a medium size round cookie cutter to cut cookies. Bake about 10 minutes at 350°F.

N o t e s :

Apple Perishky

You can substitute most fruits in this recipe.

1 lb margarine (or 1/2 butter and 1/2 margarine)

1/2 cup lard

1 cup water

1/2 cup whipping cream

1 1/2 tsp salt

1 tsp baking powder

4-6 cups flour

Put flour, baking powder, and salt in a mixing bowl. Cut in margarine and lard. Add water and cream and mix lightly to form a dough.

Refrigerate for 1 hour or more. Make apple filling with homemade applesauce, add sugar to sweeten to taste, cool. If it's watery add some minute tapioca. Roll out dough thin. Cut into 2 1/2" squares. Put applesauce in middle and bring corners to the middle and pinch together. Bake at 400°F until golden, approximately 10-15 minutes. Makes 4 dozen.

Notes :

Paska

Willard's mother's recipe. This recipe is lighter and fluffier, not quite as rich.

1 medium size potato

2 cups scalded milk

1 cup butter

1 tsp salt

1 Tbsp honey

10 whole eggs

3 cups sugar

1 1/2 Tbsp lemon or orange extract

4 Tbsp instant yeast

14 cups flour

Boil potato and put through a sieve. Add enough water to make 2 cups. Add milk, butter, salt, and honey to the potato liquid and let cool.

Beat 10 whole eggs and 3 cups of sugar until thick. Add lemon or orange extract. Set aside.

Add enough flour to the cooled liquid to make a thin batter. Take 1 cup flour from the 14 cups and mix yeast into flour and add to the soft dough with your hands until smooth. Fold in egg and sugar mixture and add to rest of flour. Work the dough and knead until smooth and elastic. Let rise to double the size and then knead a little again. Let rise to triple the size. Make into loaves or braids or whatever form you like and let rise in pan until double. Bake in 275°F oven until golden.

Notes:

Paska...continued

ICING FOR PASKA:

2 cups icing sugar

1 round Tbsp butter

1/2 tsp vanilla

Enough milk so it spreads on easy

Mix well and spread on top of Paska loaves and sprinkle with trimettes.

CHEESE SPREAD FOR PASKA:

1/2 lb Philadelphia cream cheese, room temperature

1 egg yolk

1/4 cup icing sugar

Beat until smooth and spread on Paska slices like butter.

Notes:

Grandma's Buns

DOUGH:

14-15 cups flour (1-3 cups more if needed)

4 Tbsp instant dry yeast - put into bowl with some flour
and mix well before adding to the dough.

6 cups scalded milk

ADD:

3/4 cup soft butter

3/4 cup shortening or margarine

1 round Tbsp of honey

1 1/2 Tbsp salt

Let cool to lukewarm. Use quite a large pan. Put in the mixed liquid and add enough flour to make a sponge, (soft enough so you can use an electric mixer). Then add yeast and flour mixture and work by hand.

Now really beat the dough, with electric mixer or by hand, until bubbles form on top of dough and dough is very smooth. Then add a few more handfuls of flour and mix into this soft dough by hand. Add an additional 1/4 cup of soft butter and work this into dough. Add a bit more flour to finish dough. Keep kneading dough until it lets go of your hands. Lightly oil pan with butter and put dough into pre-warmed oven. Let rise for 20 to 30 minutes, then punch down and put back into oven and let rise 3 times the size.

Pinch off dough into buns and set on pans. Let rise in warm oven, to no more than double the size or they will drop instead of rise in oven when baked. Pre-heat oven to 400°F and bake for 10 to 12 minutes. These buns freeze well. Yield: 6 dozen buns.

Fruit Platz

2 cups diced fruit – apples, rhubarb, plums etc.

4 heaping Tbsp butter

2 eggs

1 1/4 cups sugar

2 cups flour

2/3 cup boiling water

Pinch of salt

4 tsp baking powder

1 tsp vanilla

Mix butter, sugar, and eggs in mixer. Sift flour, salt, and baking powder and slowly mix alternately with boiling water. Add vanilla. Pour into greased 9"x 13" pan. Sprinkle apples or other seasonal fruit over top. Sprinkle with 1/2 cup granulated sugar and bake at 400°F for 1/2 hour.

Notes:

Neujahrskuchen (Porzelki)

This is a traditional Mennonite New Years Day fritter that is really good served hot with farmer sausage or for dessert by itself.

2 cups milk

1/2 cup shortening

2 tsp salt

2 pkgs yeast

5 eggs (beaten)

1 1/4 cups sugar

1/4 tsp nutmeg (optional)

2 cups raisins

6 1/2 cups flour

Scald milk. Add shortening and salt. Cool milk until lukewarm; then add yeast. Mix sugar with nutmeg and raisins and combine with beaten eggs. Stir into first mixture. Add enough flour to make very soft dough and knead well. Let rise in a warm place until it doubles in bulk. Drop cookies by spoonfuls into the hot fat. Deep fry until golden brown. Roll in sugar and serve warm.

N o t e s :

Perogies

This is Willard's mom's recipe. A very large recipe.

6 dry cottage cheese cartons or 2 kg cottage cheese

ADD TO THE COTTAGE CHEESE:

I dozen egg yolks

1/2 Tbsp salt

I Tbsp pepper

Mix well.

DOUGH:

I pint whipping cream

3 cups 2% milk

2 large eggs

Beat eggs, cream and milk together. Add enough flour to make a soft dough. Place dough under inverted bowl and let stand for a while, this period tends to soften and raise dough. Roll out to 1/8" thickness. Cut either into 3 inch squares or with round cutter and fill. Fold over and pinch dough into half circles or triangles.

Boil Perogies for approximately 5 minutes. Serve with applesauce or rhubarb sauce and the following cream sauce:

1/4 cup butter

1/4 cup Tbsp flour

3 cups whipping cream (or cereal cream)

I tsp salt

1/2 tsp pepper

Melt butter in saucepan. Add the flour and pour in whipping cream and salt. Boil for a few minutes until thick.

Meat Perishky

5 cups flour (approximately)

2 tsp salt

4 tsp baking powder

I cup lard

2 cups milk

FILLING:

2 lbs lean ground beef

1/2 onion finely chopped

I tsp garlic powder

2 eggs

1/4 cup bread crumbs

2 tsp salt

Mix together flour, salt, and baking powder. Cut in lard until it is coarse crumbs. Add the milk and mix together to form dough. Refrigerate for 30 minutes. Combine filling and roll into 1" meatballs. Roll out pastry until thin. Cut into 2 1/2"squares and put 1 meatball into each square. Gather the opposite corners to the middle and pinch closed. Bake at 400°F for 12 minutes or until golden brown. Serve as a sandwich substitute or with soup such as Borscht. Makes 4 dozen.

N o t e s :

Pluma Moos

This is cold fruit compote. It is delicious served with ham and fried potatoes. When I was growing up we often had it for Sunday lunch because Mom could prepare it ahead of time.

1 can pitted cherries

2 quarts water

1 cup seedless raisins

1 cup dried prunes

1/4 cup dried peaches

1/4 cup dried apricots

1/2 cup sugar

1 pkg cherry jello

4 Tbsp cornstarch

1 stick cinnamon

Wash fruit; add warm water, jello, and spices. Cook until almost tender. Prepare paste with cornstarch, sugar, and salt. Slowly add cornstarch paste, stirring constantly. Cook until slightly thickened. Cool and refrigerate. Can be made a few days ahead.

Serve warm or cold. Sweet cream may be added for extra flavour.

Notes :

Mennonite Borsht

3 quarts water

1 ring farmer sausage or 1 ham or beef bone

1/2 cabbage, shredded

4 Tbsp fresh dill

4 Tbsp fresh parsley

3 bay leaves

3 carrots, sliced

4 potatoes, chopped

2 onions, chopped

Salt – to taste

12 whole peppercorns

1/2 whole chili

14 oz can of tomatoes

1 can tomato soup

Sour cream to taste

The ingredients to this soup should be measured by how thick or thin you like soup to be. Add all the ingredients, except sour cream to the water and simmer for 1 - 1 1/2 hours, or until well done

Home Made Mustard

1 cup whipped cream

3 Tbsp dry mustard

1/4 cup sugar

Whip cream and add the mustard and sugar to taste. Serve with hot or cold ham.

SUBSTITUTIONS

Ingredient	Quantity	Substitute
Self rising flour	I cup	I cup all-purpose flour, 1/2 tsp salt, and I tsp baking powder.
Cornstarch	I Tbsp	2 Tbsp flour or 2 tsp Quick & Easy cooking tapioca
Baking powder	I tsp	1/4 tsp baking soda plus 1/2 tsp cream of tartar
Powdered sugar	I cup	I cup granulated sugar plus I tsp cornstarch blended into powder in blender
Brown sugar	1/2 cup	2 Tbsp molasses in 1/2 cup granulated sugar
Sour milk	I cup	I Tbsp lemon juice or vinegar plus sweet milk to make I cup (let stand 5 minutes)
Whole milk	I cup	1/2 cup evaporated milk plus 1/2 cup water
Cracker crumbs	3/4 cup	I cup bread crumbs
Chocolate	I sq. (I oz)	3 or 4 Tbsp cocoa plus I Tbsp butter
Fresh herbs	I Tbsp	I tsp dried herbs
Fresh onion	I small	I Tbsp instant minced onion, hydrated
Dry mustard	I tsp	I Tbsp prepared mustard
Tomato juice	I cup	1/2 cup tomato sauce plus 1/2 cup water

Ingredient	Quantity	Substitute
Catsup or chili sauce	1 cup	1 cup tomato sauce, 1/2 cup sugar, and 2 Tbsp vinegar (for use in cooking)
Dates	1 lb	1 1/2 cups dates, pitted and cut
Bananas	3 med.	1 cup mashed
Miniature marshmallows	10	1 large marshmallow

In substituting cocoa for chocolate in cakes, the amount of flour must be reduced.

Brown and white sugars: usually may be used interchangeably.

METRIC COPE CHART

Metric Cope Chart

If I can do it – you can do it! This simple list of metric working equivalents should simplify your struggle through the supermarket and help you to cope in the kitchen.

Volume Weight

Volume	Weight
1/4 tsp = 1 ml	1 oz. = 30 g
1/2 tsp = 2 ml	2 oz. = 55 g
1 tsp. = 5 ml	3 oz. = 85 g
1 Tbsp. = 15 ml	4 oz. = 115 g
1/4 cup = 50 ml	5 oz. = 140 g
1/3 cup = 75 ml	6 oz. = 170 g
1/2 cup = 125 ml	7 oz. = 200 g
2/3 cup = 150 ml	8 oz. = 250 g
3/4 cup = 175 ml	16 oz. = 500 g
1 cup = 250 ml	32 oz. = 1000 g

Measure Equivalents

1 cup = 8 oz
3/4 cup = 6 oz
2/3 cup = 5 1/3 oz
1/2 cup = 4 oz
1/3 cup = 2 2/3 oz
1/4 cup = 2 oz
1/8 cup = 1 oz

Oven Temperatures

250°F = 120°c
275°F = 140°c
300°F = 150°c
325°F = 160°c
350°F = 180°c
375°F = 190°c
400°F = 200°c
425°F = 220°c
450°F = 230°c
475°F = 240°c
500°F = 260°c